TOBACCO & HEALTH

This new series is designed to meet the growing demand for current, accessible information about the increasingly popular wellness approach to personal health. The result of a collaborative effort by a highly professional writing, editorial, and publishing team, the *Wellness* series consists of 16 volumes, each on a single topic. Each volume in this attractively produced series combines original material with carefully selected readings, relevant statistical data, and illustrations. The series objectives are to increase awareness of the value of a wellness approach to personal health and to help the reader become a more informed consumer of health-related information. Employing a critical thinking approach, each volume includes a variety of assessment tools, discusses basic concepts, suggests key questions, and provides the reader with a list of resources for further exploration.

James K. Jackson	Wellness: AIDS, STD, & Other Communicable Diseases
Richard G. Schlaadt	Wellness: Alcohol Use & Abuse
Richard G. Schlaadt	Wellness: Drugs, Society, & Behavior
Robert E. Kime	Wellness: Environment & Health
Gary Klug & Janice Lettunich	Wellness: Exercise & Physical Fitness
James D. Porterfield & Richard St. Pierre	Wellness: Healthful Aging
Robert E. Kime	Wellness: The Informed Health Consumer
Paula F. Ciesielski	Wellness: Major Chronic Diseases
Robert E. Kime	Wellness: Mental Health
Judith S. Hurley	Wellness: Nutrition & Health
Robert E. Kime	Wellness: Pregnancy, Childbirth, & Parenting
David C. Lawson	Wellness: Safety & Accident Prevention
Randall R. Cottrell	Wellness: Stress Management
Richard G. Schlaadt	Wellness: Tobacco & Health
Randall R. Cottrell	Wellness: Weight Control
Judith S. Hurley & Richard G. Schlaadt	Wellness: The Wellness Life-Style

TOBACCO & HEALTH

Richard G. Schlaadt

WELLNESS

**A MODERN
LIFE-STYLE
LIBRARY**

The Dushkin Publishing Group, Inc./Sluice Dock, Guilford, CT 06437

A AZ2085

Library of Congress Catalog Card Number: 91-072192
Manufactured in the United States of America
First Edition, First Printing
ISBN: 0-87967-877-1

Library of Congress Cataloging-in-Publication Data

Schlaadt, Richard G., Tobacco & Health (Wellness)
    1. Tobacco—Physiological effect. 2. Smoking. 3. Cigarette habit.
I. Title. II. Series.
RM666.T6   613.85   91-072192   ISBN 0-87967-877-1

Please see page 145 for credits.

The procedures and explanations given in this publication are based on research and consultation with medical and nursing authorities. To the best of our knowledge, these procedures and explanations reflect currently accepted medical practice; nevertheless, they cannot be considered absolute and universal recommendations. For individual application, treatment suggestions must be considered in light of the individual's health, subject to a doctor's specific recommendations. The authors and the publisher disclaim responsibility for any adverse effects resulting directly or indirectly from the suggested procedures, from any undetected errors, or from the reader's misunderstanding of the text.

RICHARD G. SCHLAADT

Richard G. Schlaadt was awarded his doctorate in education from Oregon State University. He has been at the University of Oregon for 24 years, 12 years as the head of the Department of School and Community Health, prior to his current appointment as Director of the University of Oregon Substance Abuse Prevention Program. He has been active in the health education area as an officer in several health organizations and the author of over 50 professional journal articles and 5 textbooks. Dr. Schlaadt sees the *Wellness Series* as the culmination of a career's work.

WELLNESS:
A Modern Life-Style Library

General Editors
Robert E. Kime, Ph.D.
Richard G. Schlaadt, Ed.D.

Authors
Paula F. Ciesielski, M.D.
Randall R. Cottrell, Ed.D.
Judith S. Hurley, M.S., R.D.
James K. Jackson, M.D.
Robert E. Kime, Ph.D.
Gary A. Klug, Ph.D.
David C. Lawson, Ph.D.
Janice Lettunich, M.S.
James D. Porterfield
Richard St. Pierre, Ph.D.
Richard G. Schlaadt, Ed.D.

Developmental Staff
Irving Rockwood, Program Manager
Paula Edelson, Series and Developmental Editor
Wendy Connal, Administrative Assistant
Jason J. Marchi, Editorial Assistant

Editing Staff
John S. L. Holland, Managing Editor
Elizabeth Jewell, Copy Editor
Diane Barker, Editorial Assistant
Mary L. Strieff, Art Editor
Robert Reynolds, Illustrator

Production and Design Staff
Brenda S. Filley, Production Manager
Whit Vye, Cover Design and Logo
Jeremiah B. Lighter, Text Design
Libra Ann Cusack, Typesetting Supervisor
Charles Vitelli, Designer
Meredith Scheld, Graphics Assistant
Steve Shumaker, Graphics Assistant
Lara M. Johnson, Graphics Assistant
Juliana Arbo, Typesetter
Richard Tietjen, Editorial Systems Analyst

THE USE OF TOBACCO has been common throughout United States history. The Native Americans used tobacco and introduced it to the European settlers. Over the years, the cigarette was developed and led to a dramatic increase in tobacco consumption. For years, it was viewed as a harmless habit.

In 1964, the first Surgeon General's report to condemn tobacco as a health hazard was published. Research started revealing how nicotine, tar, and gases from smoking (and other forms used) could cause harm to the individual. Over 25 years have elapsed since the first Surgeon General's report on smoking, and most of society has finally recognized that tobacco is hazardous to one's health. It leads to lung cancer, heart disease, strokes, emphysema, and other diseases. New research also indicates that smokeless tobacco can lead to harmful health effects. In addition, sidestream or secondhand smoking may lead to the serious illness of those who breathe the smoke.

There has been a concentrated effort to stop smoking through school and public education programs. Nonsmoking groups have protested against smokers and have been successful in establishing nonsmoking areas in restaurants, buildings, and public transportation. Various organizations like the American Cancer Society, American Lung Association, and the American Heart Association have programs designed to help smokers kick the habit. In addition are various nicotine gums, patches, and other treatments designed to help smokers taper off and quit smoking. Ultimately, the smoker must want to give up the habit in order to quit permanently; however, dependency on nicotine is very severe. Smokers often need support to give up this extremely addictive habit. Each year more and more smokers are giving up the habit. The goal of a smoke-free society by the year 2000 may be unrealistic, but Americans, albeit slowly, are approaching that goal.

This is not a definitive work, but rather a place to begin. The central objective of this book is not to make you into an instant expert on smoking and tobacco but to help you learn to *think critically* about the tobacco-related claims and counterclaims with which all of us are bombarded daily. Only then will you be able to distinguish health fact from health myth, and only then will you be an informed health consumer.

Richard G. Schlaadt
Eugene, OR

Contents

1

Smoking and You

Page 1

2

An Ancient Addiction: The History of Tobacco

Page 20

4

The Innocent Victims

Page 61

5

Prevention

Page 83

FIGURES

TABLES

CHAPTER 1

Smoking and You

Tobacco is a filthy weed: I like it.
It satisfies no normal need: I like it.
It makes you thin, it makes you lean,
It takes the hair right off your bean:
It's the worst darn stuff I've ever seen:
I like it.

Graham Hemminger (1915)

Smoking causes lung cancer, heart disease and emphysema.

U.S. Surgeon General (1989)

VIRTUALLY EVERY YOUNG ADULT hopes for—and expects to lead—a long, vigorous, and productive life. Most of us do achieve this goal, although unexpected tragedies, over which we have virtually no control, can damage or destroy this expectation. Such events—accidents, for example, or rare **genetic diseases**—are often impossible to predict and quite difficult to prevent. You can, of course, avoid getting killed in a crash by never setting foot in a car or an aircraft, but could you live a normal life with such

Genetic diseases: Illness relating to or caused by one's genes, biological elements that determine one's hereditary characteristics.

1

restrictions? And you could avoid a genetic disease only if you could choose your parents.

But you *can* take one action that will almost certainly prolong your life. This is your decision either not to start smoking or to stop if you have already started. There is no doubt that cigarettes subtract years off a normal person's life expectancy; according to recent studies, light smokers lose 4.6 years, moderate smokers 5.5 years, heavy smokers 6.2 years, and very heavy smokers 8.3 years. [1] The choice not to smoke is one that will benefit not only you, but also your family members, your friends, and even the children you may plan to have.

The decision not to start smoking is a lot easier to make than the decision to stop. Many people start smoking only because their friends or their parents smoke, because they want to feel "grown up," or because cigarette advertisements have persuaded them that smoking is sophisticated. Such influences are not too hard to resist. Even if you have smoked a cigarette or two—an experiment that almost every young person tries in the normal course of growing up—quitting need not be difficult because, if you are like most beginners, your first few cigarettes were anything but wonderful. Instead of pleasure, you probably experienced dizziness, sweating, nausea, and other kinds of discomfort. You probably persisted not for the sake of pleasure, but to be like your friends.

On the other hand, if you already smoke regularly, you will have a harder time quitting because, to put it bluntly, you have become an addict. Like the alcoholic with alcohol or the heroin addict with heroin, you have become hooked on **nicotine**, the psychoactive ingredient in tobacco. Unlike the alcoholic or the drug addict, you do not need increasing doses to produce the effect you desire. You are, however, both physically and psychologically **dependent** on tobacco and will experience a good deal of discomfort when you give it up. But, as many thousands of people demonstrate, quitting is possible—and well worth its discomfort.

THE APPEAL OF TOBACCO

Most confirmed smokers do not continue their habit solely because they are victims of a powerful addiction. There is an undeniable appeal to smoking—both **psychological** and **physiological**. Tobacco, or, more precisely, the nicotine that tobacco contains—is one of a large number of **psychoactive**, or "mood-altering," substances. This means simply that it affects your body

Nicotine: A poisonous alkaloid that is the chief psychoactive ingredient of tobacco.

Dependent: To be in need, either physically or psychologically, of regularly administered dosages of a specific substance, such as nicotine.

Psychological: Relating to the mind.

Physiological: Relating to the physical and chemical properties of living matter.

Psychoactive: Affecting mind or behavior.

(continued on p. 4)

FIGURE 1.1
Smoking Pollutes You and Everything Else

Did You Know That . . .

SMOKING
POLLUTES
YOU AND
EVERYTHING
ELSE

Tobacco use among young people has declined slowly but steadily in recent years. Whereas almost 74 percent of high school seniors had at least tried cigarettes in 1975, this figure had declined to just under 66 percent by 1989.

Source: American Cancer Society.

Smoking causes disease, shortens lives, and affects not only the smoker, but everyone with whom the smoker comes in contact.

In addition to producing short-term damage, smoking dramatically increases the risk of illness and death. Eight major studies, involving approximately 2 million people, have all found that smokers die sooner than nonsmokers. The average increase in death rate among smokers was 61 percent overall. For smokers in the two most vulnerable age groups—35 to 44 and 45 to 54—the death rates were 86 and 152 percent higher.

Smokers Die Younger

A classic study by E. C. Hammond found that the average non-smoker lives more than 8 years longer than the average very heavy smoker. Hammond's study looked at length of life in four classes of men: nonsmokers, light smokers (fewer than 10 cigarettes per day), moderate smokers (10 to 19 cigarettes per day), heavy smokers (20 to 39 cigarettes per day), and very heavy smokers (40 + cigarettes per day). Assuming that each smoker began at age 25, Hammond concluded that very heavy smokers, on average, died youngest, at age 65. Heavy smokers were the next to die—at age 67. Moderate smokers lived a year longer—they died at age 68. Light smokers died at 69. But nonsmokers lived on to the ripe old age of 73.

Thus, among the smokers in this study:

* *light* smokers gave up 4.6 years of life in exchange for smoking;
* *moderate* smokers gave up 5.5 years of life;
* *heavy* smokers gave up 6.2 years;
* *very heavy* smokers gave up 8.3 years.

These are average values and are based on studies done while most men smoked unfiltered, high-tar cigarettes. It may well be that loss of life due to smoking is somewhat less for those who smoke filtered low-tar cigarettes.

Source: Tom Ferguson, *The Smoker's Book of Health: How to Keep Yourself Healthier and Reduce Your Smoking Risks* (New York: Putnam Publishing Group, 1987), pp. 38–39.

in ways that make you feel better than—or at least different from—the way you feel before ingesting it.

Mood alteration sounds rather sinister, perhaps because we often associate it with drugs such as marijuana, cocaine, LSD, and crack. But medicine chests all over America contain completely legal mood-altering drugs prescribed by physicians—**tranquilizers**, **antidepressants**, painkillers, and other drugs that make the user "feel better." You use a mood-altering drug (caffeine) every time you drink a cup of coffee or a glass of cola. In

Tranquilizer: A substance that relaxes or calms.

Antidepressant: Medication used to relieve or prevent psychological depression.

FIGURE 1.2
Risky Substances

Mood-altering drugs include not only illegal drugs such as marijuana, cocaine, and crack, but also substances as common and readily available as alcohol, tobacco, and caffeine.

fact, many people do not feel fully "awake" until they've had their morning coffee, and some people think that they can't get through the day without six or more colas, beginning at breakfast. Tea, which also contains caffeine, has been called "the cup that cheers." Mood-altering substances are, in fact, quite common. At various times in the past, they have been even more so. Mood-altering substances such as opiates and cocaine, for exam-

FIGURE 1.3

Nicotine and the Body

Nicotine is a powerful drug that acts in the brain and throughout the body.

Readily crosses blood-brain barrier and accumulates in brain; it is faster than heroin and caffeine, for instance, but not as fast as Valium.

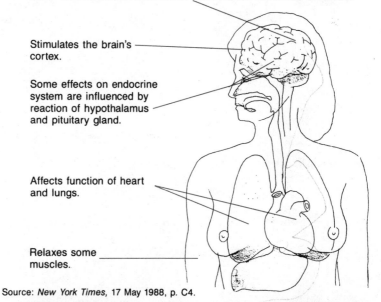

Stimulates the brain's cortex.

Some effects on endocrine system are influenced by reaction of hypothalamus and pituitary gland.

Affects function of heart and lungs.

Relaxes some muscles.

Source: *New York Times*, 17 May 1988, p. C4.

Nicotine is a chemical stimulant that affects the brain, central nervous system, and many vital organs of the body.

ple, were widely used in this country during the 19th century until the dangers associated with their use became apparent.

Nicotine is one of the most efficient mood-altering drugs the world has ever known. Many mood-altering drugs, available by prescription only, can either relax or stimulate us but not both. Tranquilizers can calm us when we're anxious. Antidepressants can make us feel better when we're down in the dumps. Nicotine, however, can act as both a stimulant and a depressant and can do much more besides. This is why smokers find that a cigarette is gratifying during a study break and also helpful in getting them through an "all-nighter." In fact, were it not for its devastating effects on health, tobacco might be recommended by physicians who now prescribe tranquilizers and antidepressants.

TOBACCO'S DANGERS

Most people who use mood-altering substances find them helpful in many situations—coffee can stimulate them for a long day of work; alcohol can relax them at a social function. But psychoactive substances have a catch: They all can damage the user's health. The health problems and high death rates of drug users and heavy drinkers are known all too well. Even such widely used substances as aspirin and caffeine can cause or worsen gastrointestinal or cardiac problems. Scientists have only recently identified and measured the extent of the severe health problems caused by smoking or chewing tobacco.

In addition to being dangerous to one's health, many mood-altering substances are **addictive**. We are all familiar with the

The Surgeon General of the United States first sounded the warning about smoking as a health hazard in 1964. Dr. C. Everett Koop, the [former] U.S. Surgeon General, named cigarette smoking "the chief preventable cause of death" and called for a smoke-free environment by the year 2000. [In May 1988], Koop declared that nicotine in cigarettes is as addictive as cocaine or heroin.

Knowing the Odds

Smoking has indeed become a hot topic with chilling statistics:

• One out of every seven deaths in this country is due to smoking. More than 350,000 deaths annually are smoking-related.

• Women who smoke will run an eight to 12 times greater risk of dying of lung cancer than nonsmokers. Lung cancer is becoming the number one cancer killer of American women, surpassing breast cancer.

• Eighty-five percent of all lung cancer deaths are due to smoking. The five-year survival rate for lung cancer patients is only 13 percent.

• Smoking is the major cause of two potentially fatal lung diseases: emphysema and chronic bronchitis.

• Smoking is one of three major risk factors for heart attack and accounts for one-third of all heart disease deaths.

• Smoking is a major cause of cancer of the throat, mouth, and esophagus and also contributes to bladder, kidney, and pancreatic cancers.

• People who smoke two or more packs a day decrease their life expectancy by more than eight years; one or more packs, six years.

• Smoking along with taking hormone-containing pills increases the risk of heart attack and stroke. Women using both cigarettes and such

Addictive: Capable of inducing a compulsive physiological or psychological need.

Did You Know That . . .

Over 1,300 Americans die each day from tobacco-related diseases.

hormones are 10 times more likely to suffer heart attacks and 20 times more likely to suffer cerebral hemorrhage than those who don't use either one.

• Infants and children of smoking parents are at increased risk of illness and death. Miscarriage, still-births, premature births, birth defects, low birth weights, and respiratory ailments in children are caused by women who smoke while pregnant.

• Good news: The percentage of adult Americans who smoke has dropped from 40 percent in 1964 to 27 percent today, according to the Centers for Disease Control. Bad news: Nearly 21 percent of high school senior girls and 18 percent of high school senior boys smoke cigarettes daily, according to the American Lung Association.

• Smoking in public places is becoming increasingly less acceptable as the dangers of breathing secondhand smoke become better documented. Sixty-seven percent of the public supports banning smoking on public airlines, while only 10 percent of the public still upholds the right of smokers to smoke anywhere.

• Each year smoking accounts for an estimated $13.8 billion in health care expenses and an additional $25.8 billion in lost wages and other costs of smoking-related illness.

• Cigarettes are the most heavily advertised product in America, according to the Chicago Lung Association. The six major cigarette companies spend about $1.5 billion on advertising each year. The United States government spends more than 10 million dollars yearly to support the tobacco industry, even while it educates people about the dangers of smoking.

Source: Ethel Gofen, "Report on Smoking: 1988," *Current Health* (November 1988), pp. 4–5.

experience of drug addicts—people who have become so dependent on the drug for their "high" that they are willing to commit crimes in order to get it. We know about alcoholics, who cannot function without a certain level of alcohol in their bloodstream. Of course, not every drinker becomes an alcoholic, and not every person who tries illegal drugs becomes an addict.

Nicotine, however, is more addictive than many of these substances. In fact, studies state that it is as addictive as cocaine and heroin. [2] Unlike the drug addict, smokers generally don't commit crimes to support their habit, and unlike alcoholics, they don't behave badly in public, lose their jobs, or suffer blackouts, but their bodies become so dependent on nicotine that giving up smoking can cause both physical and mental distress. Despite these difficulties, smokers are now kicking the habit in increasing numbers each year. In fact, nearly half of all Americans who ever smoked have quit, and about 1.3 million quit each year. Unfortunately, about 1 million young people begin smoking each year. [3]

(continued on p. 11)

Former Surgeon General C. Everett Koop has set a goal of a smoke-free society by the end of the century. He hopes to achieve this mission by seeking tough new laws that would prohibit the sale of tobacco products to minors. He noted that although 43 states already prohibit the sale of cigarettes to minors, those laws are loosely enforced. His proposals, which formed a part of the 20th annual Surgeon General's

Goals for a Smoke-Free America

report to the U.S. Congress, would include stringent licensing of tobacco vendors, a ban on coin-operated machines, and a stronger warning label on cigarette packages stressing tobacco's addictive properties.

Needless to say, a smoke-free society would be a healthier society. In addition, a decrease in premature heart attacks, cases of cancer, strokes, and emphysema would probably reduce medical expenses and lower health insurance payments. But how realistic are our chances of eliminating tobacco completely?

Since the first Surgeon General's 1964 Smoking and Health Report, more than 43 million Americans have quit smoking. According to recent estimates, this development has saved more than 200,000 lives. The number of smokers in this country has decreased from about 78 million at the time of the 1964 study to 47 million today. A smaller percentage of American adults smoke today than at any other time since the Great Depression. Researchers who base their projections on National Health Surveys conducted from 1974 to 1985 estimate that if America continues current trends, 22 percent of Americans will be smoking by the end of the century. This would mean that the number of smokers will have decreased by almost 50 percent since the 1964 Surgeon General's report.

But as heartening as this may sound, there remain some disturbing statistics that merit attention. The percentage of women smokers has not declined as rapidly as that of male smokers, and experts estimate that at the current rate female smokers will outnumber male smokers by 1995. Likewise, fewer black people have quit smoking than have white people, and the number of blacks who smoke has not diminished as quickly as that of whites. If this trend continues, black smokers will surpass white smokers by the year 1995.

Nevertheless, most of the news regarding tobacco consumption is good. There is no reason not to believe that with education, awareness, and specific programs we can become a smoke-free society—if not by 2000, then soon after.

Table 1.1 Cigarette Smoking Among American Adults, 1965, 1976, 1983, and 1987

[Data are based on household interviews of a sample of the civilian noninstitutionalized population]

Sex, Race, and Age	Current Smoker[1]				Former Smoker			
	1965	1976	1983	1987	1965	1976	1983	1987
Male				Percent of Persons				
20 years and over, age adjusted	52.1	41.6	35.4	31.5	20.3	29.6	31.1	31.4
20 years and over, crude	52.4	41.9	35.7	31.7	20.5	28.9	29.5	30.1
20–24 years	59.2	45.9	36.9	31.1	9.0	12.2	9.1	7.8
25–34 years	60.7	48.5	38.8	34.8	14.7	18.3	19.8	17.4
35–44 years	58.2	47.6	41.0	36.6	20.6	27.3	27.5	28.1
45–64 years	51.9	41.3	35.9	33.5	24.1	37.1	40.1	40.1
65 years and over	28.5	23.0	22.0	17.2	28.1	44.4	48.1	53.4
White:								
20 years and over, age adjusted	51.3	41.0	34.7	30.7	21.2	30.7	32.0	32.6
20–44 years	58.5	46.8	38.8	34.3	16.9	20.5	20.5	20.4
20–24 years	58.1	45.3	36.1	31.6	9.6	13.3	9.7	8.3
25–34 years	60.1	47.7	38.6	33.8	15.5	18.9	20.5	18.1
35–44 years	57.3	46.8	40.8	36.2	21.5	28.9	27.8	29.3
45 years and over	44.4	35.0	30.1	26.3	26.1	40.5	44.1	46.6
45–64 years	51.3	40.6	35.0	32.4	25.1	38.1	41.2	41.6
65 years and over	27.7	22.8	20.6	16.0	28.7	45.6	49.9	55.1
Black:								
20 years and over, age adjusted	59.6	50.1	42.6	40.3	12.6	20.2	23.2	22.2
20–44 years	67.7	57.4	41.8	41.3	8.3	10.2	15.4	12.9
45 years and over	52.3	42.3	42.9	39.5	17.0	30.0	30.6	32.0
Female								
20 years and over, age adjusted	34.2	32.5	29.9	27.0	8.2	13.9	16.4	18.0
20 years and over, crude	34.1	32.0	29.4	26.8	8.2	13.8	16.2	17.9
20–24 years	41.9	34.2	37.5	28.1	7.3	10.4	10.8	10.5
25–34 years	43.7	37.5	32.6	31.8	9.9	12.9	13.8	15.6
35–44 years	43.7	38.2	33.8	29.6	9.6	15.8	17.1	19.4
45–64 years	32.0	34.8	31.0	28.6	8.6	15.9	18.6	20.7
65 years and over	9.6	12.8	13.1	13.7	4.5	11.7	18.7	19.8
White:								
20 years and over, age adjusted	34.5	32.4	29.8	27.3	8.5	14.6	17.2	18.9
20–44 years	43.3	36.8	34.3	30.5	9.6	14.2	15.2	17.2
20–24 years	41.9	34.4	37.5	29.4	8.0	11.4	11.6	11.5
25–34 years	43.4	37.1	32.2	31.9	10.3	13.7	15.1	16.9
35–44 years	43.9	38.1	34.8	29.2	9.9	17.0	18.0	20.6
45 years and over	25.1	26.7	23.6	22.7	7.4	14.6	19.2	20.9
45–64 years	32.7	34.7	30.6	29.0	8.8	16.4	19.0	21.4
65 years and over	9.8	13.2	13.2	14.0	4.5	11.5	19.5	20.2

Black:								
20 years and over, age adjusted	32.7	34.7	32.5	27.9	5.9	10.2	10.7	13.2
20–44 years	45.0	40.1	36.2	32.7	5.9	8.1	7.7	8.9
45 years and over	20.6	28.3	28.1	22.7	6.0	12.4	13.4	17.4

[1]A current smoker is a person who has smoked at least 100 cigarettes and who now smokes; includes occasional smokers.

NOTE: Excludes unknown smoking status.

Source: *Health United States,* No. 0052, 1988, p. 96.

This table shows smoking percentages during three decades. All cigarette consumption has diminished significantly since 1965, but the trends are more dramatic among men than women, and among whites than blacks.

KNOWING THE DANGERS

People have recognized for centuries the damages that most mood-altering drugs can cause. Almost 200 years ago, Americans were so wary of the terrible effects of alcohol on heavy drinkers and their families that they made public drunkenness a criminal offense. People were more aware of the social damages that alcohol causes, such as disorderly conduct and violence, than of the physiological effects, such as **cirrhosis** of the liver and other alcohol-related diseases, that we know about today.

Cirrhosis: A degenerative liver disease characterized by the accumulation of large fatty deposits and scar tissue that impair functioning.

Smoking as Compared With Other Risks

The United States Surgeon General has described smoking as the "chief, single, avoidable cause of death in our society and the most important public health issue of our time." Just how does smoking stack up against other habits and conditions of modern living? As you can see from the chart below, smoking is far and away responsible for more deaths than any of these other causes. The second and third causes of death—alcoholic beverages and motor vehicles—would have to be combined to equal the number of tobacco-related deaths.

The largest category of cigarette deaths is cardio-vascular, including heart attacks and strokes. Cancer deaths—lung, as well as larynx, oral cavity, esophagus, urinary bladder, kidney and pancreas—are the second largest category of tobacco-related deaths.

Interestingly, the U.S. population does not perceive smoking to be this great a danger. Members of business and professional clubs ranked smoking fourth as a health risk—behind handguns, motorcycles and motor vehicles. College students ranked smoking third, after nuclear power and handguns.

CHART FOLLOWS

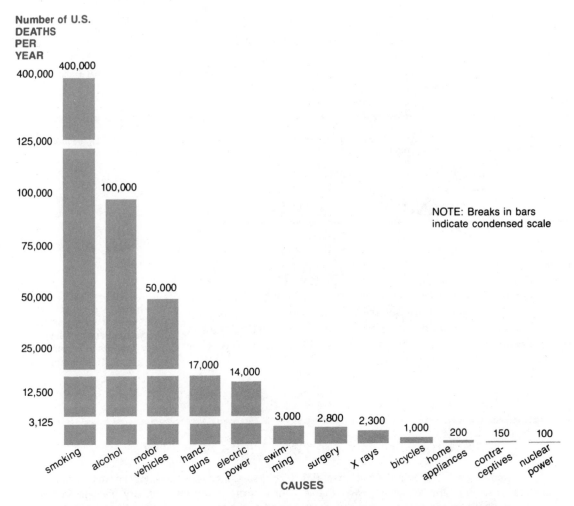

**Number of U.S.
DEATHS
PER
YEAR**

NOTE: Breaks in bars
indicate condensed scale

Source: "Clearing the Clouds," *Smokeless*, Booklet II (American Institute for Preventive Medicine, 1983), p. 15.

Epidemiologist: A scientist who researches the effects of disease on groups of people rather than individuals.

Similarly, people have suspected the dangers of smoking for a very long time, but scientists could not accurately measure the full extent of the damage smoking causes until public health agencies were able systematically to collect health statistics on very large numbers of people through birth certificates, hospital records, and death certificates. Once this information became available, **epidemiologists**—statisticians who specialize in tracking public health—were able to analyze it and discover the full and frightening extent of the health problem. Once their alarm-

FIGURE 1.4
The Serpent Cigarette

SWELL STRUGGLING WITH THE CIG'RETTE POISONER.

Source: Bettmann Archive.

This English cartoon from the 1880s illustrates that people have long suspected the dangers of smoking. However, it wasn't until accurate methods of testing and statistical information became available that government and various health groups began to seriously discourage smoking.

ing figures were published, the government and various health groups began taking serious measures to discourage smoking.

One of the most frightening discoveries epidemiologists made came in the 1920s, when they found a very strong link between smoking and lung cancer. A two-pack-a-day smoker, they found, was 22 times more likely than a nonsmoker to die of lung

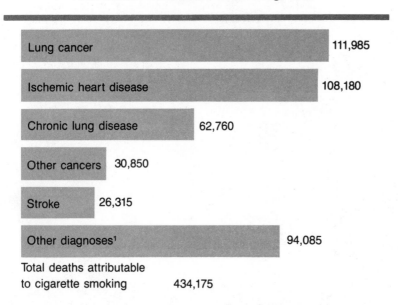

FIGURE 1.5
U.S. Deaths Attributable to Smoking, 1988

Lung cancer	111,985
Ischemic heart disease	108,180
Chronic lung disease	62,760
Other cancers	30,850
Stroke	26,315
Other diagnoses[1]	94,085

Total deaths attributable
to cigarette smoking   434,175

[1]Includes deaths from rheumatic and pulmonary heart disease, cardiac arrest, hypertension, atherosclerosis, aortic aneurysm, other arterial diseases, respiratory tuberculosis, pneumonia, influenza, low birth weight, respiratory distress syndrome, newborn respiratory conditions, sudden infant death syndrome, burn deaths, and passive smoking deaths.

Source: Office on Smoking and Health, Centers for Disease Control, Rockville, MD.

Statistics do not lie. Cigarette smoking currently accounts for over 400,000 deaths annually in the United States. The American Cancer Society estimates that smoking accounts for 30 percent of cancer deaths in this country and approximately 83 percent of lung cancer deaths. Overall, cigarette smoking was implicated in approximately 20 percent of all deaths in the United States in 1988.

cancer, and even a smoker who used less than half a pack a day was 5 times more likely to get the disease. In fact, 85 to 90 percent of people dying from lung cancer turned out to have been smokers. [4]

As frightening as lung cancer is, it is not the only disease linked to smoking. Heavy smokers are three times more likely than nonsmokers to suffer a heart attack, and even light smokers increase their chances by one and one-half times. Smokers are more likely to suffer **emphysema**, an often-fatal lung disease, and are at greater risk of developing nose and throat ailments.

Emphysema: A severe lung disorder characterized by gradual destruction of the tiny air sacs in the lung (alveoli) and a reduction in elasticity of lung tissue that impairs the lung's efficiency.

In addition to dying younger, smokers have increased rates of both acute and chronic illnesses. The U.S. Public Health Service has estimated that cigarettes are responsible for:

- 81 million missed days of work per year;
- 145 million days spent ill in bed every year;
- 11 million additional cases of chronic illness per year;

Smokers Have More Illnesses

- 280,000 additional cases of heart disease;
- 1 million additional cases of chronic bronchitis and emphysema;
- 1.8 million additional cases of chronic sinus problems;
- 1 million additional cases of peptic ulcer.

Source: Tom Ferguson, *The Smoker's Book of Health: How to Keep Yourself Healthier and Reduce Your Smoking Risks* (New York: Putnam Publishing Group, 1987), p. 39.

Did You Know That . . .

When all the data from numerous studies are pooled, it appears that living with a smoker increases the risk of dying from heart disease by about 30 percent.

They are also more likely to miss work because of illness and have a higher chance of being involved in accidents on the road or at work. [5]

DAMAGE TO OTHERS

Many people believe that smokers do damage only to themselves; this is untrue. The illnesses and injuries smokers suffer are costly to all Americans. When smokers get sick—which they do more frequently than nonsmokers—all of us share the cost of their illnesses. Almost all the hospital bills smokers compile are paid not by them but by our health insurance companies or our taxes. The high cost of treating smoking-related illnesses raises health insurance premiums and taxes for everyone.

Perhaps more distressing is the mounting evidence on the dangers of **passive smoking**. Recent studies include "Environmental Tobacco Smoke," published by the Committee on Passive Smoking at the National Research Council in 1986; "The Health Consequences of Involuntary Smoking: A Report of the Surgeon General," also published in 1986; and "Reducing the Health Consequences of Smoking: 25 Years of Progress: A Report of the Surgeon General," published in 1989. These studies indicate that smokers injure not only their own health but also the health of

(continued on p. 19)

Passive smoking: The inhalation of sidestream smoke by a nonsmoker exposed to another person's cigarette.

Why Do You Smoke?

Here are some statements made by people to describe what they get out of smoking cigarettes. How *often* do you feel this way when smoking them? Circle one number for each statement. For an accurate score, be sure you answer every question.

		ALWAYS	FREQUENTLY	OCCA-SIONALLY	SELDOM	NEVER
A.	I smoke cigarettes in order to keep myself from slowing down	5	4	3	2	(1)
B.	Handling a cigarette is part of the enjoyment of smoking it	5	4	3	2	(1)
C.	Smoking cigarettes is pleasant and relaxing	(5)	4	3	2	1
D.	I light up a cigarette when I feel angry about something	(5)	4	3	2	1
E.	When I have run out of cigarettes I find it almost unbearable until I can get them	(5)	4	3	2	1
F.	I smoke cigarettes automatically without even being aware of it	5	4	3	2	(1)
G.	I smoke cigarettes to stimulate me, to perk myself up	5	4	3	2	(1)
H.	Part of the enjoyment of smoking a cigarette comes from the steps I take to light up	5	4	3	2	(1)
I.	I find cigarettes pleasurable	(5)	4	3	2	1
J.	When I feel uncomfortable or upset about something, I light up a cigarette	(5)	4	3	2	1
K.	I am very much aware of the fact when I am not smoking a cigarette	5	4	3	(2)	1
L.	I light up a cigarette without realizing I still have one burning in the ashtray	5	4	3	2	(1)
M.	I smoke cigarettes to give me a "lift"	5	4	3	2	(1)
N.	When I smoke a cigarette, part of the enjoyment is watching the smoke as I exhale it	5	4	3	2	(1)
O.	I want a cigarette most when I am comfortable and relaxed	5	4	(3)	2	1
P.	When I feel "blue" or want to take my mind off cares and worries, I smoke cigarettes	(5)	4	3	2	1
Q.	I get a real gnawing hunger for a cigarette when I haven't smoked for a while	5	4	3	2	(1)
R.	I've found a cigarette in my mouth and didn't remember putting it there	5	4	3	2	(1)

How to Score

1. Enter the numbers you have circled to the smoking questions in the spaces below, putting the number you have circled to question A over line A, to question B over line B, and so on.

2. Total the 3 scores on each line to get your totals. For example, the sum of your scores over lines A, G, and M gives you your score on *Stimulation*—lines B, H, and N give the score on *Handling,* etc. Scores can vary from 3 to 15. Any score 11 and above is *high;* any score 7 and below is *low.*

				TOTALS
1	+ 1	+ 1	=	3
A	G	M		STIMULATION
1	+ 1	+ 1	=	3
B	H	N		HANDLING
5	+ 5	+ 3	=	13
C	I	O		PLEASURABLE RELAXATION
5	+ 5	+ 5	=	15
D	J	P		CRUTCH: TENSION REDUCTION
5	+ 2	+ 1	=	8
E	K	Q		CRAVING: PSYCHOLOGICAL ADDICTION
1	+ 1	+ 1	=	3
F	L	R		HABIT

What Your Scores Mean

What kind of smoker are you? What do you get out of smoking? What does it do for you? This test is designed to provide you with a score on each of six factors that describe many people's smoking. Your smoking may be well characterized by only one of these factors, or by a combination of factors. In any event, this test will help you identify what you use smoking for and what kind of satisfaction you think you get from smoking.

The six factors measured by this test describe one or another way of experiencing or managing certain kinds of feelings. Three of these feeling-states represent the *positive* feelings people get from smoking: (1) a sense of increased energy or *stimulation,* (2) the satisfaction of *handling* or manipulating things, and (3) the enhancing of *pleasurable feelings* accompanying a state of well being. The fourth is the *decreasing of negative feelings* by reducing a state of tension or feelings of anxiety, anger, shame, etc. The fifth is

a complex pattern of increasing and decreasing "craving" for a cigarette, representing a psychological *addiction* to cigarettes. The sixth is *habit* smoking, which takes place in an absence of feeling and is purely automatic smoking.

A score of 11 or above on any factor indicates that this factor is an important source of satisfaction for you. The higher your score (15 is the highest), the more important a particular factor is in your smoking and the more useful the discussion of that factor can be in your attempt to quit.

A few words of warning: If you give up smoking, you may have to learn to get along without the satisfactions that smoking gives you. Either that or you will have to find some more acceptable way of getting this satisfaction. In either case, you need to know just what it is you get out of smoking before you can decide whether to forego the satisfactions it gives you or to find another way to achieve them.

Stimulation If you score high or fairly high on this factor, it means that you are one of those smokers who is stimulated by the cigarette—you feel that it helps wake you up, organize your energies, and keep you going. If you try to give up smoking, you may want a safe substitute, a *brisk walk* or moderate exercise, for example, whenever you feel the urge to smoke.

Handling   Handling things can be satisfying, but there are many ways to keep your hands busy without lighting up or playing with a cigarette. Why not toy with a pen or pencil? Or try doodling. Or play with a coin, a piece of jewelry, or some other harmless object. There are plastic cigarettes to play with, or you might even use a real cigarette if you can trust yourself not to light it.

Accentuation of Pleasure—Pleasurable Relaxation   It is not always easy to find out whether you use the cigarette to feel *good,* that is, get real, honest pleasure out of smoking or to keep from feeling so *bad.* About two-thirds of smokers score high or fairly high on *accentuation of pleasure,* and about half of those also score as high or higher on *reduction of negative feelings.*

Those who do get real pleasure out of smoking often find that an honest consideration of the harmful effects of their habit is enough to help them quit. They substitute eating, drinking, social activities, and physical activities—within reasonable bounds—and find they do not seriously miss their cigarettes.

Reduction of Negative Feelings, or "Crutch"   Many smokers use the cigarette as a kind of crutch in moments of stress or discomfort, and on occasion it may work; the cigarette is sometimes used as a tranquilizer. But the heavy smoker, the person who tries to handle severe personal problems by smoking many times a day, is apt to discover that cigarettes do not help him deal with his problems effectively.

When it comes to quitting, this kind of smoker may find it easy to stop when everything is going well, but may be tempted to start again in a time of crisis. Again, physical exertion, eating, drinking, or social activity—in moderation—may serve

as useful substitutes for cigarettes, even in times of tension. The choice of a substitute depends on what will achieve the same effect without having any appreciable risk.

"Craving" or Psychological Addiction   Quitting smoking is difficult for the person who scores high on this factor, that of *psychological addiction.* For him, the craving for the next cigarette begins to build up the moment he puts one out, so tapering off is not likely to work. He must go "cold turkey." It may be helpful for him to smoke more than usual for a day or two, so that the taste for cigarettes is spoiled, and then isolate himself completely from cigarettes until the craving is gone. Giving up cigarettes may be so difficult and cause so much discomfort that once he does quit, he will find it easy to resist the temptation to go back to smoking because he knows that some day he will have to go through the same agony again.

Habit   This kind of smoker is no longer getting much satisfaction from his cigarettes. He just lights them frequently without even realizing he is doing so. He may find it easy to quit and stay off if he can break the habit patterns he has built up. Cutting down gradually may be quite effective if there is a change in the way the cigarettes are smoked and the conditions under which they are smoked. The key to success is becoming *aware* of each cigarette you smoke. This can be done by asking yourself, "Do I really want this cigarette?" You may be surprised at how many you do not want.

Summary

If you do not score high on any of the six factors, chances are that you do not smoke very much or have not been smoking for very many years. If so, giving up smoking—and staying off—should be easy. If you score high on several categories, you apparently get several kinds of satisfaction from smoking and will have to find several solutions. Certain combinations of scores may indicate that giving up smoking will be especially difficult. Those who score high on both *reduction of negative feelings* and *craving* may have a particularly hard time in going off smoking and in staying off. However, there are ways to do it; many smokers represented by this combination have been able to quit.

Others who score high on Factors 4 and 5 may find it useful to change their patterns of smoking and cut down at the same time. They can try to smoke fewer cigarettes, smoke them only half-way down, use low-tar-and-nicotine cigarettes, and inhale less often and less deeply. After several months of this temporary solution, they may find it easier to stop completely. You must make two important decisions: (1) whether to try to do without the satisfactions you get from smoking or find an appropriate, less hazardous substitute, and (2) whether to try to cut out cigarettes all at once or taper off. Your scores should guide you in making both of these decisions.

Source: Daniel Horn and Associates, *A Self-Test for Smokers* (Test 3), DHEW Publication No. (CDC) 75-8716 (Washington, DC: Public Health Service, Department of Health and Human Services, 1983).

those who spend time with them at close quarters, including spouses, children, office mates, and even people sharing the same car, aircraft, or other vehicle for long periods of time. For this reason, many state governments have passed laws prohibiting smoking in stores, offices, public buildings, and commercial aircraft. For more on passive smoking, see chapter 4.

The 1986 Environmental Smoking report and the legislation resulting from it are only the latest developments in the long saga of tobacco use. In fact, the history of tobacco comprises much more than medical findings and government actions. Throughout the ages, tobacco has served as a religious tool, as a fashion statement, as a taxable commodity, and even as a medicine. It has attracted thousands of advocates and opponents, including explorers, kings, soldiers, and politicians, and addicted millions more. Chapter 2 explores the history of tobacco and details its journey through Western culture. ▨

An Ancient Addiction: The History of Tobacco

TOBACCO'S HISTORY is as rich and colorful as that of the cultures it has influenced. It is also an age-old one, for humans were smoking, chewing, and sniffing tobacco hundreds of years before Columbus discovered America. The battle we are now fighting for a smoke-free nation is against an old nemesis—a drug whose addictive properties have enticed us for centuries.

EARLY HISTORY

In November 1492, two men Christopher Columbus had sent ashore from his ship anchored off the coast of Cuba reported to their commander that they had come across natives holding and puffing on a lighted firebrand. One month after the discovery of the New World, this was the first contact European natives had with what was an ancient Native American custom: smoking tobacco. Perplexed by the notion of inhaling and exhaling smoke, the explorers initially concluded that the natives were perfuming themselves with the lighted herb. Eventually they understood that the custom was an essential part of many North American Indian social and religious rituals. [1]

Tobacco was, indeed, an important facet of ancient American Indian culture; myths abounded concerning the herb's origin. According to one legend, during a great famine, when all the lands were barren, a goddess descended from a great cloud to save the people. Where she touched the ground with her right hand, maize grew. Her left hand brought kidney beans and potatoes.

FIGURE 2.1
Indian Ritual Smoking

Source: Culver Pictures, Inc.

Many North American Indian tribes believed tobacco to be a gift from the gods and used it for both religious and therapeutic purposes.

Where she sat, tobacco grew. Whether the tobacco was intended as a gift, along with the vegetables, or as a message, signifying that the gift of food was not without a price, is unclear, but the Indians quickly became addicted to this magical herb, and smoking it was considered a sacred act. [2]

A PRECIOUS HERB

Believing that smoking held both supernatural and medicinal properties, the Indians utilized tobacco for both religious and **therapeutic** purposes. Long ceremonies filled with prayers,

(continued on p. 24)

Therapeutic: Having properties that cure or treat disease.

Potent from the First Ancient Puff

SUMMARY: Research is producing intriguing insights into the neuropharmacological properties of nicotine. Yet much remains to be learned about the alkaloid that has borne tobacco to profound influence in such varied reaches as shamanistic ritual, colonial rule and handling today's stress.

To shamans of certain South American Indian tribes, tobacco was the nourishment of the supernaturals. It is romantically portrayed in the porticoes of the U.S. Capitol as a tribute to its prominent role in the economy. To the surgeon general, it is the leading cause of preventable death. Nonetheless, it holds nearly 30 percent of the U.S. population in thrall. Tobacco would be but a humble weed were it not for the presence of nicotine.

Nicotine is among the most prominent members of the chemical family of alkaloids, compounds that plants make to ward off insects and other herbivores. Caffeine is another alkaloid. It is easy to see why nicotine is such a compelling drug. "People use it to alert themselves and at other times to calm themselves," says Dr. Darrell G. Kirch, medical director of the Neuropsychiatric Research Hospital of the National Institutes of Mental Health in Washington. Smoked with shallow puffs, a cigarette becomes a stimulant; deep puffs render it a relaxant.

Though the data are somewhat equivocal, there is evidence that nicotine helps people concentrate on boring, repetitive tasks and, alternatively, to calm themselves in the face of stress or to wind down after a hard day at the office. As Dr. Ovide F. Pomerleau, a professor of psychiatry at the University of Michigan, has said, "Smoking is the ideal drug for the puritan ethic."

But years before cigarette smoke began to billow through the offices of the United States of the postagricultural era, the taking of tobacco through the lungs, the skin and the gastrointestinal tract and the experiencing of its powerful effects gained religious significance among South American tribes.

Among certain tribes, nicotine was part of the initiation ritual for new shamans. Initiates would take large doses rectally, in conjunction with hallucinogens, says Johannes Wilbert, author of the 1987 book "Tobacco and Shamanism in South America." The nicotine would paralyze the respiratory system and suppress color vision at the same time, and the new shamans would come back from the brink of death convinced they had seen the underworld, he says. The elder shamans rarely lost an initiate from overdose; they were skilled pharmacologists taking advantage of the speed with which nicotine is excreted, so that the poisoning was quite transient.

Columbus was the first European to learn about tobacco and its uses. Various explorers took it to Europe, where its use spread widely during the 16th century. Nicotine got its name from Jean Nicot, counselor to the king of France, who introduced tobacco into his country in 1560.

At that time, many countries strictly forbade the use of tobacco, with penalties of mutilation and death in Turkey, Russia and China, says Andrew Weil, author of "From Chocolate to Morphine," a guide to mind-altering drugs. Some of this prohibition was motivated by a reputation as the recreation of deviants, and some had to do with political economics: To the British, tobacco meant revenue for Spain—until the acquisition of the Virginia colonies.

The subjective benefits of nicotine are legion. In a 1982 survey by the American Cancer Society, 87.5 percent of smokers reported that smoking was pleasurable. Nicotine may improve long-term memory, according to Pomerleau and his wife, psychologist Cynthia S. Pomerleau, in their 1984 paper, "Neuroregulators and the Reinforcement of Smoking: Towards A Biobehavioral Explanation," which is regarded as the classic in the field. "Smoking/nicotine administration has been shown to improve visual surveillance, reaction time, mental efficiency, and rapid information processing . . . especially on monotonous tasks," they found. Not surprisingly, then, office workers smoke at a rate 30 percent higher on the job than off, they found.

Some, however, dispute the notion that smoking improves performance. Smoking has effects that would reduce general performance, such as reducing the blood's ability to carry oxygen to the brain, says Jack E. Henningfield, a laboratory chief in the addiction research center of the National Institute on Drug Abuse. And there is no way, he adds, to compare a smoker's performance with what it would have been had he or she never smoked.

Studies in animals and humans suggest that smoking relieves anxiety. Smokers, the Pomerleaus write, "smoke more when anxious or when subjected to painful stimulation . . . before giving a lecture, during doctoral examinations, receiving electric shocks, etc." Twenty percent of smokers report that they smoke partly to control weight, and studies have shown that smokers weigh on average several pounds less than nonsmokers. Nicotine also appears to raise one's threshold of pain.

But sorting the myriad effects of this drug is proving a daunting task. "Nicotine goes everywhere and does everything, which is part of what makes it such a fascinating drug," says Kirch. Nicotine's effects are so pervasive that it was used to map the nervous system around the turn of the century, says Henningfield.

Nicotine derives its broad range of effects from its molecular mimicry of acetylcholine, a neurotransmitter (a chemical that nerve cells use to communicate with one another). There are many neurotransmitters, most of which operate in specific systems within the brain or nervous system, but acetylcholine is ubiquitous. To complicate matters, nicotine affects other transmitter systems, as well as hormonal systems, in ways that are only beginning to be understood. For example, any or all of several neural pathways may be responsible for its reported effects on alertness. Nicotine causes the release of adrenal hormones. Nicotine receptors are found in an area of the brain stem responsible for wakefulness

called the reticular activating system, as well as in the cerebral cortex, where higher thought processes take place.

And nicotine causes the pituitary gland to secrete the hormone vasopressin, which is thought to enhance both learning and memory. (Vasopressin also causes constriction of blood vessels.) Additionally, "Nicotine receptors [which are a major type of acetylcholine receptor] have been identified in the cerebral cortex and in the hippocampus, which is clearly involved in memory formation," says Dr. Paul A. Newhouse, professor of psychiatry at the University of Vermont College of Medicine. That nicotine may be acting at these sites to improve cognitive function is a matter of speculation. "If I could prove it," he says, "I could win the Nobel Prize."

As for relieving anxiety and promoting pleasure, there is some evidence that nicotine stimulates the production of endorphins, opiates produced in the brain. For example, one study showed that naloxone, an opiate blocker sometimes used to treat drug addicts, blocked the pleasurable effects of smoking. Henningfield claims another study failed to show this effect and that mecamylamine, a nicotine blocker, is much more effective.

Henningfield says the pleasure of smoking is mediated "at least in part through the dopamine system." The dopamine transmitter system is thought to mediate the satisfaction people obtain from performing life's tasks, from eating to sex to a job well-done. Drugs of abuse, such as heroin and cocaine, are pernicious because they short-circuit the dopamine system, giving a person an overdose of pleasure in the absence of achievement.

Obviously, nicotine does not overwhelm the dopamine system in the manner of cocaine and heroin. But several observations raise tantalizing questions about nicotine's role. "A lot of patients with psychiatric disorders smoke," including 90 percent of schizophrenics, says Kirch. In fact, the drive to smoke is so strong among schizophrenics that at the Neuropsychiatric Research Hospital, where smoking is otherwise forbidden, schizophrenics are allowed to smoke, says Jules

Asher, a spokesman for the mental health institute.

Furthermore, researchers have observed a peculiar association of schizophrenia and Parkinson's disease. Both diseases involve disorders of the dopamine system, and a possible relationship between nicotine and motor problems. Schizophrenics who smoke are more likely than nonsmoking schizophrenics to develop a disorder of involuntary movements called tardive dyskenesia. "This involves an excess of dopamine," says Kirch. Parkinson's patients have too little dopamine in their brains. Smokers are less likely than nonsmokers to develop Parkinson's. "Certain kinds of patients may gravitate toward nicotine, perhaps in an attempt to treat their symptoms," Kirch says. But exactly how nicotine might be affecting the dopamine system and these diseases remains unclear.

Like Parkinson's disease, Alzheimer's involves a loss of acetylcholine receptors in the brain. Alzheimer's patients whom Newhouse has treated with nicotine have had mild improvements in thinking, but "with a strong negative effect on mood."

Intriguingly, nicotine has been found to alter the concentrations of acetylcholine receptors in certain parts of the brain. Studies by Kenneth J. Kellar, professor of pharmacology at Georgetown University School of Medicine, first demonstrated this effect in rats. Later, autopsies in Scotland found excess receptors in the brains of smokers, and now, brain scans in Sweden of living smokers have found the same thing, using positron emission tomography. But the significance of this, like that of many of nicotine's effects on humans, remains very much a matter of speculation.

Is nicotine itself a hazard to health when smoked? Animal studies suggest that it may play a role in peptic ulcer disease and in the induction and aggravation of cardiovascular disease. Its constriction of the blood vessels might be responsible for the latter. Although nicotine is not a carcinogen, a few of its metabolic breakdown products are. Like its neuropharmacology, nicotine's effects on the rest of the body are only beginning to be outlined.

—David Holzman

Source: David Holzman, *Insight* (8 May 1989), pp. 50–51.

chanting, and sometimes animal sacrifices featured tobacco as an integral tool to help the Indians summon and communicate with sacred spirits. Tribal leaders inhaled vast amounts of lit tobacco, then fell into a trance and experienced religious visions.

The religious significance tribespeople attached to tobacco must have convinced them that the plant had some therapeutic value, for the Indians used tobacco to treat an infinite number of maladies, ailments, and illnesses. The ways the Indians extracted the medicinal ingredient from the plant were as varied as the diseases they hoped to cure: They heated the leaves and applied them to diseased parts of the body; they wrapped a leaf around a pill and swallowed both; they mashed the leaf and mixed it with sugar and water to concoct a syrup; and sometimes they simply smoked it.

The Indians also used tobacco to stave off thirst and hunger. To serve this purpose, they combined powdered tobacco with moistened, burned shells from the river to form a pill that they swallowed as needed. South American tribes in Peru and Venezuela sniffed mashed tobacco to halt **epilepsy**, treat colds, and relieve headaches. The Zuni Indians treated victims of rattlesnake bites by first sucking the wound to remove the poison and then exhaling tobacco smoke all over the sufferer's body to ease the pain. [3]

One other therapeutic use of tobacco involved eating the plant. This was less a medicinal practice than a purification device and was reserved solely for adult men and women. If a group of Indians were uncomfortable after having overindulged in a bit too much dinner, one of them might eventually suggest that perhaps everyone should eat a bit of tobacco. After pounding and grinding the leaf into a fine powder, then moistening it and placing the concoction on a pestle, the Indians, one by one, took tastes of the mixture from the pestle. After a few minutes, the Indians quietly and politely left the gathering to throw up, bathe, and retire for the night. [4]

ON TO EUROPE

About 100 years after Columbus's initial discovery, tobacco arrived in Europe. In about 1560 the Spanish physician Francesco Hernandez visited Mexico and brought tobacco seeds back to the king of Spain, Philip II. A year later a French lord bought the plant at a Portuguese marketplace (from a Flemish merchant who had journeyed to Florida) and presented it to his country's queen, Catherine de Medici. These certainly were royal introductions for such a harmful substance. At this time nobody knew of smoking's dangers, and many physicians believed, as the Indians had, that tobacco had significant therapeutic properties. These physicians freely prescribed tobacco as medicine.

In the meantime, smoking was becoming an increasingly fashionable habit in England. Explorer and colonist Sir Francis Drake is usually credited with being the first to bring tobacco to his native country, in 1570. His fellow countryman, Sir Walter Raleigh, courtier and favorite of Queen Elizabeth I, returned from the colony of Virginia an established smoker. He was one of the first noblemen to engage in the pastime; his manservant was so aghast at seeing his employer exhale smoke that he threw a mugful of ale over Raleigh's head in an effort to extinguish the fire. Raleigh, too, was convinced of the plant's medicinal value; he claimed that smoking promoted good health among the Virginia colonists and among Indians in the New World.

Did You Know That . . .

The Puritans of colonial Massachusetts and Connecticut were the first to impose bans on tobacco in America. They claimed tobacco caused sloth and immorality, as well as physical and mental illness.

Epilepsy: A disorder characterized by disturbed electric impulses in the central nervous system.

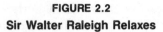

FIGURE 2.2
Sir Walter Raleigh Relaxes

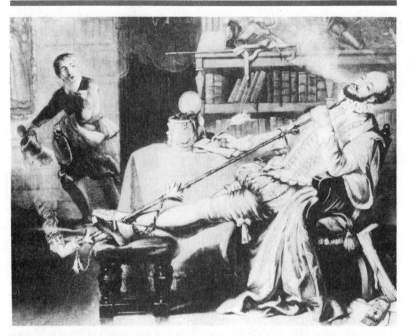

Source: Bettmann Archive.

Sir Walter Raleigh's servant was so startled when he saw his master smoke that he threw a mugful of ale on Raleigh's head in order to put out the fire.

TAXING THE CROP

As tobacco's popularity grew in England, so did concern about its health hazards. One of the earliest antismoking campaigners was King James I, who believed that smoking tobacco was not only dangerous but downright immoral. In 1604 King James issued a proclamation prohibiting tobacco planting anywhere in England and Wales. This new legislation served the king well in two ways: First, it prevented English farmers from planting what James had concluded was a substance "crude, poisonous, and dangerous for the bodies and health of our subjects." [5] Second, it enabled the king to tax the crop's importation—the first of many taxes government leaders would place on tobacco.

The king's tax notwithstanding, the British continued to smoke tobacco, and, in some areas, to grow it illegally. Tobacco continued to prosper in Europe as the seventeenth-century progressed. **Snuff**, richly perfumed tobacco sniffed through the nose, became quite the vogue in France during the reign of Louis XIV. The king himself disapproved of the habit (his father had as well, going so far as to decree that tobacco could be sold only by doctor's prescription; the new policy was vastly unpopular and was eventually revoked). But noblemen and noblewomen in Louis's court (snuff was an upper-class practice) carried silver boxes containing the precious herb. When **bubonic plagues** ravaged London in 1665 and Vienna in 1679, people smoked vast amounts of tobacco as a medicinal—and preventive—measure. Schoolboys at Eton, England's exclusive boys' school, had to smoke tobacco every morning to protect themselves from the disease. [6] The crop also became a rich source of revenue as kings and princes continued to tax its importation and sale heavily.

Taxing tobacco became a major money-making strategy a century later in the newly independent United States. Taxing this substance, along with liquor and various imports, helped the U.S. government fund the War of 1812. At about this time, a new mode of smoking became fashionable. Cigars (called *cigarros* in Spanish), resembling the firebrands that native Indians smoked, gradually replaced the long clay pipes most people had used to smoke tobacco during its early European history. Cigars became more popular than either pipe tobacco or snuff.

There were few limitations on smoking during the late eighteenth and early nineteenth centuries, and the habit was tremendously popular. Clergymen smoked. Schoolboys smoked. One doctor endorsed the habit for women, claiming that "[it] is a glorious venture when a woman takes heart to smoke . . . tobacco. Her charming sex has an equal right with men." [7] Governments lifted all restrictions on tobacco, until the only regulations that remained concerned possible fire hazards.

EARLY ANTISMOKING MOVEMENTS

There were, however, those in both Europe and the United States who failed to fall under tobacco's magnetic spell. Queen Victoria of England loathed the habit and tried to outlaw it in the British army—an unsuccessful venture indeed. In America the health advocate Sylvester Graham (1794–1851; he is better known for inventing the Graham cracker) stressed **abstinence** from both

---

Did You Know That . . .

President James Madison referred to tobacco products as one of the "pleasures of life" and refused to place a luxury tax on them.

Snuff: A plug of tobacco specifically prepared for inhalation through the nose.

Bubonic plague: A contagious, deadly disease characterized by uncontrolled lymph node swelling.

Abstinence: The total avoidance of a specific substance, such as alcohol or tobacco.

tobacco and alcohol in his writings concerning health. Others feared that smoking tobacco led inevitably to an increased consumption of alcohol; it was these **temperance** workers who led the first antismoking demonstrations in the United States in the 1830s. [8]

The antismoking movement gained some momentum over the next couple of decades as proponents linked tobacco to a host of conditions, from cancer and heart disease (an accurate assessment) to constipation, acne, and baldness (not quite as precise). In the 1850s the more timely issues of slavery and secession placed antismoking sentiment on a back burner as the country headed for civil war.

CIGARETTES AND ANTISMOKING MOVEMENTS

During this time a new smoking tool emerged that would replace cigars as the most popular tobacco instrument. This was the cigarette, which originated in Brazil in the early 1800s. By the middle of the nineteenth century, cigarettes had become popular in Spain, France, and then the United States. The U.S. government taxed cigarettes for the first time in 1864, but at that time 1884 more Americans smoked cigars or chewed tobacco. Twenty years later, however, cigarette manufacturers hit upon a gold mine that would increase cigarette sales many thousandfold and raise the ire of a new antismoking movement. This new invention, the cigarette machine, could produce 200 cigarettes a minute, or 120,000 in a 10-hour day. This mass production drove the price of cigarettes down and sent sales sky high.

This tremendous sales increase did indeed spark a new crusade against tobacco. Leaders of the new movement rallied around some new claims about the dangers of cigarettes. Some of these reports—the hazards cigarettes cause for passive smokers (a foreshadowing of the 1986 Surgeon General's report; see chapter 4), for example—were accurate. Others, such as rumors that cigarettes were laced with **opium**, were misleading. All of them spurred more widespread antismoking sentiment, and cigarettes were dubbed "coffin nails." Lobbyers petitioned Congress to require that cigarette packages be labeled "poison." Some employers began refusing to hire smokers. States drew up statutes prohibiting the sale of cigarettes to minors. [9] Beginning in 1893 with Washington, fourteen states outlawed tobacco smoking entirely.

Temperance: Avoidance of, or moderation in the use of, a mood-altering substance.

Opium: A bitter brown narcotic drug that comes from the dried juice of the opium poppy, and from which narcotics such as heroin and morphine are derived.

(continued on p. 31)

In the 1800s, Antismoking Was a Burning Issue

When U.S. Surgeon General C. Everett Koop declared in May 1988 that cigarettes were as addictive as cocaine and heroin, he was echoing sentiments that had been expressed more than a hundred years earlier. As the author of one anti-tobacco tract put it in 1877, "So powerful are the charms of this foul narcotic that health and long life are sacrificed to it by millions." The *New York Times* reflected prevailing attitudes when it editorialized in 1884 that the "decadence of Spain began when the Spaniards adopted cigarettes and if this pernicious practice obtains among adult Americans the ruin of the Republic is close at hand."

Life has never been easy on Tobacco Road. The state legislators who passed anticigarette laws in the late 19th and early 20th centuries were members of a large fraternity of kings, emperors, popes and potentates who have tried, at various times and in various ways, to wean their constituents from Lady Nicotine. The first recorded legal proceeding against a smoker was initiated on ecclesiastical grounds in the 15th century. When Rodrigo de Jerez, a member of Christopher Columbus' expedition who apparently learned to smoke in Cuba, lit up for the first time back home in Spain, the townspeople—alarmed by the smoke issuing from his mouth and nose—assumed he had been possessed by the devil. He was promptly imprisoned by the Inquisition. King James I considered tobacco and papism to be among the biggest evils facing his realm. Several popes agreed with him, at least on the first point. Pope Innocent X and Pope Urban VIII excommunicated smokers.

Excommunication was the least of a smoker's worries in the 17th century. In China, an imperial edict issued in 1638 made the use or distribution of tobacco a crime punishable by decapitation. Sultan Ahmed I of Turkey reportedly ordered the noses of smokers to be pierced with pipestems. His son and eventual successor, Murad IV, took an even harder line: he had smokers executed as infidels. In Russia, smokers were flogged; the nostrils of repeat offenders were slit; persistent violators were exiled to Siberia. In Persia, they were tortured, impaled and/or decapitated.

The first organized antitobacco movement in the United States began in the 1830s. It was supported largely by temperance workers, who argued that smoking dried out the mouth, creating a "morbid or diseased thirst" that could be satisfied only by the whiskey jug or the brandy bottle. The readers of one antitobacco tract were taken on a visit to the Realm of Satan, where Prime Minister Tobacco assisted King Alcohol in evil deeds.

The "sot weed" also attracted the attention of early health reformers. Sylvester Graham, whose name has been immortalized by the Graham cracker, included abstinence from tobacco and alcohol in his blueprint for health, as did advocates for such diverse medical dogmas as hydropathy, phrenology and eugenics. Joel Shew, a promoter of hydropathy ("the water cure"), counted 87 diseases caused by smoking, including cancer, heart disease, constipation, acne, insanity and tooth decay. Tobacco faced a lengthy list of other indictments. It was unnatural, unclean, unwholesome, unrefined, unattractive, ungentlemanly and messy. It caused baldness. It exhausted the soil. It was a waste of money. It fostered pauperism and crime and a "horrid train" of other social problems. It had "ruinous effects" on morality. Some reformers said that the moral decay sprang from physical deterioration; others that tobacco attacked the conscience directly. At any rate, it was agreed that smoking was associated with indolence, licentiousness, profanity and the reading of novels, among other signs of depravity.

Tobacco had its defenders, of course. The argument that it was an "accursed tributary" leading to drink was countered by the claim that it promoted temperance. Many writers, both physicians and laymen, recommended smoking for health. Belief in the healing power of tobacco dates back to the 16th century. Tobacco, unknown in the Old World, was widely distributed in the New. Since native Americans enjoyed uncommonly good health compared with Europeans at the time of contact, it seemed logical that they were being protected by something in their environment. An enthusiastic clan of physicians, sailors, scholars and quacks built a body of faith around tobacco, incorporating it in the treatment of an almost-inclusive list of health problems. Although the luster of tobacco as a panacea faded in the 18th century, it continued to be included in the materia medica until well into the 20th century. Many Victorian physicians believed that the heated smoke of a cigarette, pipe or cigar would kill germs. Both the popular and the scientific press carried periodic reports about the effectiveness of smoking as a disinfectant and prophylactic.

The antitobacco campaign lost its momentum during the mid-1850s, when the growing conflict over slavery overshadowed other social issues. With the outbreak of the Civil War, the crusade vanished almost entirely from public view. By the 1880s, however, antismoking forces had regrouped, in response to the threat posed by a new enemy: the cigarette. . . .

The cigarette was a tempting target in part because it was relatively new, and thus less entrenched than the banker's cigar or the farmer's pipe. It was also faintly subversive, a symbol of disturbing change, associated with cities and immigrants. New York City alone accounted for 25 percent of the cigarette sales between 1895 and 1910. Machine-made cigarettes were popular with immigrants. Expensive hand-rolled brands continued to be smoked by daring members of the upper classes. Middle-class reformers from the xenophobic hinterland tended to hold suspect the habits of the foreign-born, the wealthy and the citified. . . .

The case against cigarettes included the charge that they were unhealthy, even fatal. They were associated with heart disease, respiratory problems, birth defects and most of the other diseases now linked to smoking. The major exception was lung cancer, which was very rare until the 1930s, and not even recognized as a disease until 1923. The warnings about the haz-

ards of smoking do not appear to have been taken very seriously, however, perhaps because they did not have the endorsement of the medical establishment. As late as 1948, the *Journal of the American Medical Association* was arguing that "more can be said in behalf of smoking as a form of escape from tension than against it . . . there does not seem to be any preponderance of evidence that would indicate the abolition of the use of tobacco as a substance contrary to the public health." . . .

Efforts to curb smoking by minors served as the opening wedge in the legislative campaign against cigarettes. By 1890, according to one tally, 26 states and territories had outlawed the sale of cigarettes to minors (defined as anything from age 14 to 24). Mindful of the sanctity of the family, a number of states stipulated that cigarettes could be sold or given to minors with parental consent. Penalties for violating the laws varied widely, with the average being a fine of $20–25. . . .

In 1892, the reformers petitioned Congress to prohibit the manufacture, importation and sale of cigarettes. The Senate Committee on Epidemic Diseases concluded that only the states had such authority. The committee, however, agreed that cigarettes were a public health hazard and urged the petitioners to seek remedies from state legislatures. By the end of the decade, four states had outlawed the sale of cigarettes to adults as well as minors. The campaign escalated in 1899 when a Chicago group backed by business interests organized the Anti-Cigarette League, which was headed by the indefatigable Lucy Page Gaston—the Carry Nation of cigarettes. By 1901, the league claimed a membership of 300,000, with a paid staff overseeing chapters throughout the United States and Canada. . . .

World War I provided the nails for the coffin of the first anticigarette movement. Increased prosperity, the demands of the military and the spread of cigarette smoking among women combined to strengthen the industry while weakening the opposition. Military commanders had long regarded tobacco as essential for the fighting man. "Tobacco is as indispensable as the daily ration," Gen. John J. (Black Jack) Pershing, commander in chief of the American Expeditionary Force, cabled Washington, D.C. "We must have thousands of tons of it without delay." Americans from all walks of life responded to the call. Theaters set up boxes to collect pennies from children and cigarettes from smokers. Celebrities by the score pronounced tobacco a necessity for the defense of democracy. The campaign to send smokes Over There even reached into prisons, where inmates gave up their tobacco rations in the interest of besting the Hun. By the time Johnny came marching home, the once disreputable cigarette had become an almost unassailable symbol of courage, decency and the American Way. . . .

The cigarette had won the first round. But out of the ashes, as it were, of the old movement has come a new campaign. By the 1980s, states were once again passing antismoking laws; government agencies were issuing restrictive regulations; and the courts were busy with cigarette-related litigation. For much of middle-class America, the cigarette had become a social liability. Smokers retreated to the back of the plane, the back stairs at the office, the back porch at the dinner party. The release of the 1988 Surgeon General's Report on Smoking and Health, equating cigarettes with heroin and opium, brought the movement full circle. No doubt the report would have been taken as vindication by the Rev. M. R. Drury, who predicted a century ago that "the time is not far distant when the use of tobacco will be generally looked upon with disfavor and admit of no apology whatever." On the other hand, an Italian physician may have been closer to the mark when he observed, in 1713, that "This vice will always be condemned and always clung to."

Source: Cassandra Tate, *Smithsonian* (July 1989), pp. 107–117.

THE TWENTIETH CENTURY

During World War I, new wealth, military demands, and a marked increase in smoking among women drove tobacco sales up again. Smoking was especially widespread among the armed forces, who considered cigarettes nearly as essential to the war effort as their weapons. Laws against tobacco were repealed and controls lifted.

In the 1920s, scientific evidence linking smoking to disease began to appear as medical journals reported more cancer, more heart disease, and a lower life expectancy among smokers than among nonsmokers. As potentially jarring as these new studies were, they did next to nothing to slow down the momentum cigarette smoking had gained during the war years. New findings notwithstanding, cigarette consumption doubled in the years between 1920 and 1930. Cigarettes were in such demand during World War II that draft boards ordered **deferments** for tobacco farmers. [10] Cigarette advertisements were responsible for much of the continued success of tobacco during the early twentieth century, as they featured prominent celebrities such as sports

Deferment: Official postponement of military service.

(continued on p. 33)

Ladies First

In decades past, smoking by women was considered to be a social taboo. It was unladylike and unattractive; something better left to men, who were ushered into the parlor to smoke by themselves after dinner.

Times changed. When women started to smoke, particularly after World War II, they took to it with a vengeance. Tobacco companies, then as now, created advertising that equated smoking with strength, fun, independence, adventure, and glamour. Lighting up became a mark of liberation.

A Deadly Match

A funny thing happened on the way to the cigarette machine. Although medical literature had, in fact, documented this a decade earlier, it was not until the early 1950's that word started to leak out that smoking was dangerous. Even deadly. Doctors were warning patients about the risk of lung cancer. Men began to put their cigarettes out once and for all. Women didn't listen. Instead, they began smoking in greater numbers.

In 1964, Surgeon General Luther Terry confirmed everyone's fears with his landmark report stating that cigarette smoking was "hazardous to your health," a phrase that was imprinted on every American-made pack of cigarettes distributed in the United States. This information created so much concern among men who smoked that 20 percent decided to end their habit before their habit put an end to them. In contrast, the number of female smokers increased.

The shift in numbers created a level of equality among male and female smokers that would have given their grandmothers the vapors. Both sexes were smoking in nearly equal numbers. But whereas men were showing a healthy fear of cigarettes—then called "cancer sticks" and "coffin nails"—women acted as though they were immune from harm. They weren't.

The Numbers Speak for Themselves

Over the past twenty years, studies have clearly established that women are subject to the same ill effects from smoking as men. From 1950 to 1980, lung cancer rates among females increased more than 400 percent. By 1985, lung cancer became the most common form of cancer found in women, surpassing breast cancer.

The self-destruction that women who smoke heap upon themselves doesn't stop at lung cancer and other diseases of the pulmonary system. Add to this list the risks of coronary disease, severe hypertension, hardening of the arteries and stroke—disorders that are more common among women who smoke than among those who don't.

Smoking also gravely affects the female reproductive system. Women smokers have a threefold greater risk of developing cervical cancer than female non-smokers. Pregnant smokers face additional risks. Each puff increases their chances of suffering miscarriages, premature births, smaller than normal full-term babies and prenatal deaths.

In spite of these compelling reasons to quit smoking or never start at all, women continue to light up: the fastest growing group of smokers in the United States is women under age 23. The fates of these women are made bleaker by the fact that women have greater difficulty quitting smoking than men.

The Most Encouraging Development in Recent Years Is the Emergence of a Powerful Anti-Smoking Movement.

Female Focus

Advertising by tobacco companies exploits the smoking phenomenon among women. Even a quick study of cigarette advertisements shows how tobacco companies are doing everything they can to manipulate women most vulnerable to smoking. Virtually no ad features a woman over 25 years old. Tobacco companies know that older females are either hooked already or not interested. Ad after ad is targeted at young women. They are the most susceptible to the lures manufactured by Madison Avenue, plus they have the greatest potential of becoming lifelong customers.

Advertising isn't the only way tobacco companies appeal to women. The Virginia Slims Championships of women's tennis is perhaps the most brilliant example of market positioning aimed at women in the history of the tobacco industry. The best in women's tennis travel to 60 tournaments around the country each year to participate in this $1,000,000 event, the richest in women's tennis. The result? To young girls nationwide, the brand Virginia Slims is linked to tennis icons such as Steffi Graf, Martina Navratilova, Chris Evert and Gabriela Sabatini—women who don't smoke.

Changing Habits

Although many fronts are working diligently to maintain the fateful marriage between women

and tobacco, women need not be victims. Young women must work harder at resisting the temptation to start smoking. Women who are habitual smokers must remember that addictions can be broken. It takes determination, will-power and—most of all—a desire to live.

The most encouraging development in recent years is the emergence of a powerful anti-smoking movement. Our increasingly health-conscious society has taken heed, endorsing efforts to curtail and even prohibit smoking in public places. Hopefully, society's stand against smoking will help accelerate the downward spiral for this product, which is lethal when used as intended. Otherwise, females will have the dubious distinction of being not only the leaders of the pack, but of the whole carton.

—Dr. Zira De Fries

Source: Zira De Fries, *Priorities* (Winter 1990), pp. 24–25.

---

stars; tobacco companies also geared much of their advertising campaigns toward female smokers, whose numbers continued to increase.

EVIDENCE AND ACTION

In the 1950s, antismoking movements found new supporters as doctors used the increasing evidence to form a new crusade, including in their ranks the U.S. surgeon general. In 1960 the American Cancer Society concluded "beyond reasonable doubt" [11] that cigarette smoking caused lung cancer. In 1964 the U.S. Surgeon General's Advisory Committee released *Smoking and Health,* which concluded that cigarette smoking was a primary cause of lung cancer, emphysema, chronic **bronchitis**, and heart disease.

The message about tobacco finally seemed to ring clear. One month after the Surgeon General's report was released, the Federal Trade Commission issued a ruling limiting cigarette advertising, and 5 years later all cigarette commercials were banned from both television and radio. Cigarette sales dropped 20 percent in the first 2 months following the report's publication. [12] Ciga-

Bronchitis: Acute or chronic inflammation of the bronchial tubes.

(continued on p. 35)

FIGURE 2.3
Cigarette Advertising

Source: Culver Pictures, Inc.

Advertising campaigns that made smoking look romantic and glamorous were particularly effective in attracting women to take up smoking.

FIGURE 2.4
Smoke Signals

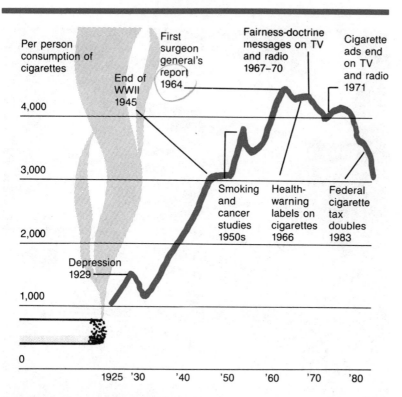

Per person consumption of cigarettes

End of WWII 1945

First surgeon general's report 1964

Fairness-doctrine messages on TV and radio 1967–70

Cigarette ads end on TV and radio 1971

4,000

3,000

Smoking and cancer studies 1950s

Health-warning labels on cigarettes 1966

Federal cigarette tax doubles 1983

2,000

Depression 1929

1,000

0

1925 '30   '40   '50   '60   '70   '80

Note: Per capita consumption is based on persons 18 years and older.
Figures for last two years are subject to revision.

Source: *U.S. News & World Report*, 23 January 1989, p. 9. Basic data: Department of Agriculture, Department of Health and Human Services.

Smoking consumption has significantly decreased since publication of the first surgeon general's report in 1964.

rette smokers in the United States have decreased from 40 percent of the adult population in 1965 to 29 percent in 1987. [13] Moreover, the 1986 Surgeon General's report on the dangers of passive smoking (see chapter 4) has prompted new policies limiting smoking in restaurants, offices, airplanes, and trains.

Today, cigarette packages must carry warnings stating that cigarette smoking is a health hazard. The American Cancer

FIGURE 2.5

Surgeon General's Warnings

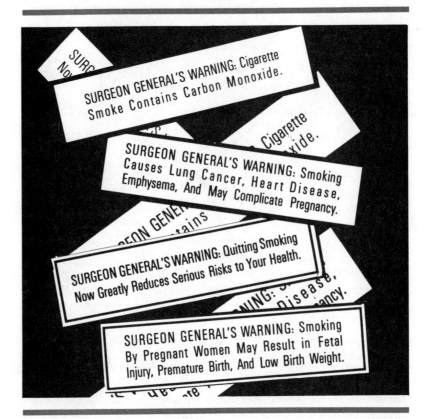

SURGEON GENERAL'S WARNING: Cigarette Smoke Contains Carbon Monoxide.

SURGEON GENERAL'S WARNING: Smoking Causes Lung Cancer, Heart Disease, Emphysema, And May Complicate Pregnancy.

SURGEON GENERAL'S WARNING: Quitting Smoking Now Greatly Reduces Serious Risks to Your Health.

SURGEON GENERAL'S WARNING: Smoking By Pregnant Women May Result in Fetal Injury, Premature Birth, And Low Birth Weight.

Two years after the surgeon general's report was published in 1964, warning labels became mandatory on cigarette packages. The first such label stated that "smoking may be hazardous to your health." The current warning labels are much more explicit.

Society, the American Heart Association, and the American Lung Association have all started new campaigns changing the focus of their battle against lung disease to prevention, a goal that will entail stronger efforts to educate people about the dangers of smoking. [W]

3

Physiology and Health Hazards

NICOTINE is a tremendously powerful drug. It can produce both awareness and relaxation. It is easily accessible and relatively inexpensive. Along with these pleasurable properties, nicotine and its fellow components in cigarettes, smokeless tobacco, cigars, and pipes have toxic, often harmful effects upon the human body. The ways in which these substances influence bodily function and their long-term consequences are the focus of this chapter.

PHYSIOLOGY

Cigarette smoke contains hundreds of chemical substances. Three of the most damaging of these are nicotine, **tar**, and **carbon monoxide**. Nicotine is found in the root of the tobacco plant. When it is fresh, it is a colorless oil; it turns brown when exposed to air. Tar results from **organic** matter burned in the presence of air and water at a sufficiently high temperature. Because it requires such a high temperature, it is not present either in unburned tobacco or in chewing tobacco or snuff. Carbon monoxide is a gas produced by burning material. The amount of carbon monoxide increases in places where little oxygen is present—the motor of an automobile, the workings of a gas stove, and the inside of a cigarette.

Nicotine
Pharmacologically, nicotine is categorized as a **stimulant** because it provokes **nerve cells** in the brain and heightens awareness. Its effects are so complex, however, that no one classification is completely accurate. For example, nicotine stimulates certain

Tar: A solid residue formed when the particles in tobacco smoke condense. Cigarette tar is made up of several hundred different chemicals.

Carbon monoxide: A colorless, odorless toxic gas present in some engine exhaust and cigarette smoke.

Organic: Of, relating to, or derived from living organisms.

Stimulant: A substance that increases either muscular activity or nerve activity in the brain.

Nerve cell: Neuron; the fundamental functioning unit of nervous tissue.

FIGURE 3.1
The Smoking Cycle

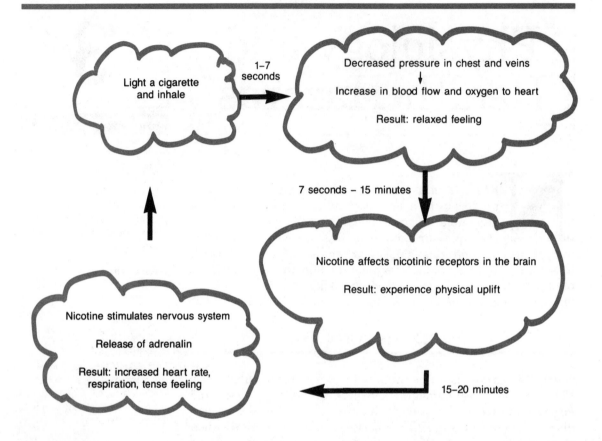

Source: "Taking Off," *Smokless,* Booklet I, American Institute for Preventive Medicine, 1990, p. 11.

Lighting up and inhaling a cigarette causes immediate changes in the smoker's body.

nerves in the spinal cord known as Renshaw cells. This effect, in turn, relaxes many nerves in the body and slows down certain reactions, such as knee reflexes. The drug's effects also depend on the amount in the body. For example, some nerve cells are stimulated by a small amount of nicotine but depressed by large amounts of the drug.

One can ingest nicotine by smoking (cigarettes), chewing (chewing tobacco), or inhaling (snuff). Chewed or inhaled nicotine enters the **circulatory system** through the **mucosae** (thin skin) of the nose or mouth. It then travels through **capillaries** contained in the mucosae to the bloodstream, which in turn carries it to the brain. When it is smoked, nicotine goes through the **alveoli** (air cells) of the lungs into the arterial bloodstream, which carries it directly to the brain. The entire process takes less than 10 seconds.

Once in the brain, nicotine stimulates neurons by imitating the behavior of a **hormone** called **epinephrine** (adrenaline) and **acetylcholine**, a **neurotransmitter**. A person's body naturally releases epinephrine when he or she is anxious or under stress. Scientists believe that acetylcholine may play a major role in the nerve centers for thought and higher mental functions (some research indicates that some of the symptoms of **Alzheimer's disease**, a progressive illness marked by severe loss of memory, may be caused by a depletion of neurons that use acetylcholine). [1] At the same time that nicotine mimics these two chemicals, which heighten awareness, it triggers the release of **endorphins**, the brain's natural opiates, which produce a calming effect. As a result, many smokers experience a simultaneous feeling of excitement and relaxation while nicotine is in their bloodstreams.

Tar

Tar is one of the most dangerous components of cigarette smoke. When a person inhales from a burning cigarette, tar contained in the smoke fills the alveoli of the lungs. Over time this effect can lead to respiratory problems, such as bronchitis and emphysema, as well as contributing to the development of lung cancer. Cigarette companies are aware of these dangers and have lessened the amount of tar in some of their brands. This action has been mildly successful, but because tar is so integral to both the flavor and satisfaction of a cigarette, some smokers either avoid low-tar brands completely or, when they use them, inhale so deeply that they ingest almost as much tar—and more of other hazardous chemicals—as when they smoke their regular brand. This defeats the purpose of using a low-tar brand in the first place.

Carbon Monoxide

Carbon monoxide (CO) is chemically similar to **carbon dioxide** (CO_2). Produced by normal body processes, carbon dioxide travels through the lung alveoli into the bloodstream, where it bonds

(continued on p. 41)

Circulatory system: The system consisting of the heart and blood vessels which transports blood throughout the body.

Mucosae: Another name for the mucuous membranes that line many internal body cavities and passages.

Capillary: A vessel that carries blood between the arteries and veins.

Alveoli: Tiny air sacs in the lungs.

Hormone: A chemical released into the bloodstream by a gland to produce a specific effect on certain bodily tissue.

Epinephrine: A natural hormone, also known as adrenaline; triggered by stress, exercise, or fear.

Acetylcholine: A type of neurotransmitter that is thought to play a role in the nerve centers for thought and higher mental function.

Neurotransmitter: The chemical that transmits messages between neurons.

Alzheimer's disease: A degenerative disease of the central nervous system, characterized by prematurely senile mental deterioration.

Endorphins: A group of substances produced within the body that relieves pain.

Carbon dioxide: A colorless, odorless gas present in air and produced as a by-product of the bodily metabolic process.

Smoke Gets in Your Heart

Of all pollutants, carbon monoxide is one of the most pervasive, both indoors and outdoors. Any fire, be it from a cigarette tip, an automobile engine, a gas stove, or a kerosene space-heater, generates carbon monoxide. High levels of this gas, as everyone knows, are fatal. But what about the lower levels typical of freeways and smoke-filled meeting rooms?

Carbon monoxide poisoning is really asphyxiation—oxygen deprivation. The invisible, odorless gas attaches firmly to hemoglobin, the red pigment of blood, where it occupies portions of the molecule normally available to transport oxygen from the lungs to the rest of the body.

When 50–80% of the hemoglobin becomes blocked by carbon monoxide, the brain dies, and if the build-up has been rapid there may be very little warning. If the level rises more slowly, 30–50% of the hemoglobin may be blocked with little more than flu-like symptoms the result. A more rapid rise to such high levels causes headache, dizziness, confusion, and nausea. When the level is at 2–4%, which is common for many people in everyday situations, the symptoms are relatively subtle, though unpleasant. Impairment of thinking and fine motor coordination has been observed. New research shows that even at these levels, the heart is also affected.

Intrigued by earlier reports of impaired cardiac function, Dr. Thomas Dahms of the St. Louis University School of Medicine and a team of associates set out to learn whether fairly typical levels of carbon monoxide impaired the ability of people with heart disease to exercise. For their research, they selected 63 nonsmoking men between the ages of 35 and 75. All the men had proven coronary artery disease, which made them vulnerable to angina during exercise. With limited circulation to the heart, these men were expected to be very sensitive to reduced oxygen delivery.

Each subject was asked to exercise on a treadmill while his heart's response was monitored by an electrocardiograph machine. During exercise, the men breathed either room air or air with added carbon monoxide. When carbon monoxide displaced only 2% of the blood's oxygen, the subjects' ability to exercise was measurably impaired. At 4%, chest pain ended the workout sooner than if the subjects were breathing room air. In a telephone interview, Dr. Dahms commented on a surprising aspect of these findings: "People with more severe coronary disease were no more susceptible to the effects of carbon monoxide than people with lesser disease." Nor did a patient's age and medications influence the outcome.

In daily life, 2% of the oxygen-carrying capacity of blood is easily lost. This is the level reached by a nonsmoker who spends time in a room with cigarette smokers. A commuter on a busy highway can easily reach 4%; in one study, travelers on a Los Angeles freeway averaged 4.9%. A pack-a-day smoker is routinely at the 4% level. Firefighters battling a blaze, tunnel workers, waiters in a smoky bar or restaurant, and many other people who work in an industrial or factory setting are also likely to run levels in this range. And carbon monoxide isn't confined to work sites. Wood-burning stoves and kerosene heaters can generate significant amounts of the gas if they are badly designed or installed. Cars with defective exhaust systems, even on lonely country roads, can raise blood levels of carbon monoxide into this range.

It is somewhat unusual for the average person to exercise hard while also inhaling carbon monoxide, but that is deceptive. It takes over 5 hours for the carbon monoxide level in blood to fall by one-half. The person who leaves a smoky business meeting and walks several blocks, the commuter who climbs a few flights of stairs after getting out of his or her car—these people are exercising with less than a full deck of oxygen.

As Dr. Dahms remarks, his study "has some import for setting air pollution standards." The Environmental Protection Agency currently puts a 2% level of carbon monoxide in the blood at the upper limit of the acceptable range. A 4% level can result from workplace exposures meeting the standards of the Occupational Safety and Health Administration. But, as Dr. Dahms's data show, such levels are hardly healthy for people with limited coronary reserve. The new research "provides a solid basis for the claim that there are definite adverse health effects," when 4% of hemoglobin is carrying carbon monoxide. Given the pervasiveness of carbon monoxide in the environment, these results suggest that standards should be reviewed and, probably, revised.

Source: *Harvard Medical School Health Letter,* Vol. 15, No. 5, March 1990, pp. 4–5.

with **hemoglobin** to form **carboxyhemoglobin** (COHb). Hemoglobin is the blood component that removes carbon dioxide from the body and carries oxygen into the body. Carbon monoxide also arrives in the bloodstream through the alveoli, and like carbon dioxide it then bonds with hemoglobin. But carbon monoxide bonds much more tightly and, therefore, leaves the body much more slowly. In the meantime, the blood accumulates much higher amounts of carbon monoxide. This action can slowly starve the body of oxygen. An insufficient amount of oxygen can affect heart functioning; in extreme cases it can cause a heart attack.

According to studies, people who smoke one pack per day have carbon monoxide levels in their bloodstreams of 25 to 35 parts per million blood components. However, even these "moderate" smokers may have levels of 100 p.p.m. for short periods of time. In general, levels of carbon monoxide in the blood of smokers are 4 times higher for moderate smokers than for nonsmokers and often as much as 15 times higher for heavy smokers.

Hemoglobin: The oxygen-carrying pigment found in red blood cells.

Other Components

Researchers have devised cigarette-smoking machines to collect and study cigarette smoke, which is composed of both gases and solids. Cigarette smoke contains more than 4,000 substances. The machine can separate the gas and solid phases through a filter, which traps particles larger than one micrometer and stores the rest (gas) in a special tank. These machines are designed to smoke a cigarette the way a typical smoker would.

During a puff, the tip of the cigarette's burning end reaches a temperature of nearly 2,000 degrees Fahrenheit. This tiny furnace activates the organic (leaves, paper, sugar, nicotine) and inorganic (water, tar, metal, radioactive elements) materials. The cigarette filter and paper act to filter **mainstream smoke** before the smoker inhales it. The cigarette does not filter **sidestream**

Carboxyhemoglobin: A combination of hemoglobin and carbon monoxide, which forms in the blood when carbon monoxide is inhaled so that the blood is unable to combine with oxygen.

Mainstream smoke: The smoke from a cigarette inhaled only by the smoker.

Sidestream smoke: The smoke that escapes from the tip of the cigarette; can be inhaled by nonsmoking bystanders.

(continued on p. 43)

Table 3.1 Harmful Substances in Cigarette Smoke

About 4,000 chemical compounds are produced when tobacco burns. The following constituents of cigarette smoke are known or suspected to be harmful to the human body:

acetaldehyde
acetone
acetonitrile
acrolein
acrylonitrile
alcohols
ammonia
amphenols
arsenic
benza(a)anthracene
benzene
benzo(a)pyrene
benzo(j)fluoranthene
benzo(g,h,i)perylene
butylamine
cadmium compounds
carbon dioxide
carbon monoxide
catechol
creols
DDT
dibenz(a,j)acridine
dibenz(a,h)acridine
dibenzo(c,g)carbazole
diethylnitrosamine
dimethylamine
dimethylnitrosamine
endrin
ethylmethylnitrosamine
fluoranthene
formaldehyde
furfural
hydrazine

hydrocyanic acid
hydrogen cyanide
naphthalenes
nickel compounds
nicotine
nitric oxide
nitriles
nitrogen oxides
N-nitrosonornicotine
nitrosopyrrolidine
polonium-210
pyrene
vinyl chloride
*   *   *

1-methylindoles
3- &4-methylcatechols
5-methylchrysene
9-methylcarbazoles
*   *   *

other acids
other catechols
other ketones
other metallic ions
other nitrogen-containing
    compounds
other nitrosamines
other phenols
other polynuclear aromatic
    hydrocarbons
other radioactive compounds
other sulfur-containing
    compounds

Source: Tom Ferguson, *The Smoker's Book of Health* (New York: Putnam Publishing Group, 1986), p. 44.

A look at the substances a person inhales every time he or she draws on a lit cigarette.

smoke, which escapes from the tip of the cigarette; this smoke results from a slightly cooler burning process than does mainstream smoke, so that the tobacco it contains has not burned completely, and the smoke is filled with more unburned particles. This sidestream smoke is hazardous not only to actual smokers but to passive smokers as well (see chapter 4).

HEALTH RISKS

Chapter 2 mentioned that since 1964 the Surgeon General has required every cigarette package to display a label warning of the dangers of cigarettes. In 1985, the warnings became more specific; the labels variously state that cigarettes contain carbon monoxide; that they can be harmful to pregnancy; that they can cause emphysema and respiratory problems; that they may be responsible for some **cardiovascular** diseases; that they cause lung cancer; or that quitting smoking reduces serious health risks. These warnings have probably had some influence on the increasing numbers of American smokers determined to quit; nevertheless, hundreds of thousands of people in the United States continue to die every year from tobacco-related diseases.

Lung Cancer

According to the American Cancer society, lung cancer accounts for more than 117,000 deaths per year. It is the cause of about 25 percent of all cancer deaths and about 5 percent of all deaths in the United States. Cigarette smoking is the leading cause of lung cancer in this country. [2]

Some of the evidence scientists have used to link cigarettes to all types of cancer is the presence of **carcinogens** in the smoke. Most of the carcinogens that cause lung cancer are the particles (as opposed to the gas) in the smoke. These include not only tar but the metals nickel and cadmium and the chemicals benzopyrene and dibenzanthracene. Part of these solids remain in the lungs after the cigarette smoke is exhaled.

The lung airways are covered by a thin layer of cells called the **epithelium**, which actually lines all human surfaces, both inside and outside the body. This cell layer absorbs cigarette smoke into the lungs soon after the smoke enters the body. At this point, components in the smoke reach the **sputum**, which is manufactured by a combination of mucus produced by cells lining the **bronchial tree** and old cells this lining has shed. Over a period of time, their presence in the sputum may cause **mutations** in the cell genes, which may lead to the formation of

(continued on p. 45)

Epithelium: One or more of the cellular layers that completely cover the surface of the body.

Sputum: A mixture of saliva combined with mucus and other substances secreted by the lining of the respiratory tract.

Cardiovascular: Of the heart and blood vessels.

Carcinogens: Cancer-causing agents.

Bronchial tree: The branched, hollow tubing that connects breathing passages from the mouth and nose to the lungs.

Mutation: A change in the DNA, the genetic material of a living cell.

FIGURE 3.2
Health Risks of Smoking

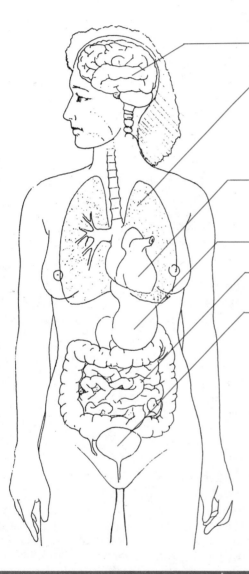

Brain: Smoking restricts oxygen flow and causes a narrowing of the blood vessels in the brain, which can lead to stroke.

Lungs: Cigarette smoke not only introduces carcinogens directly to the lung tissue, but also impairs the cilia's ability to clear these and other harmful foreign substances from the lungs, increasing the risk of lung cancer, the most deadly form of all cancers. Hydrogen cyanide and other chemicals in the smoke damage the lungs, leaving them more susceptible to infections and diseases such as emphysema, bronchitis, and pneumonia.

Heart: Nicotine increases heart rate, elevates blood pressure, and constricts the blood vessels, which can lead to a heart attack. Cigarette smoke also constributes to the buildup of fatty deposits in the arteries (atherosclerosis), and is therefore a major risk factor for heart disease.

Stomach: Cigarette smoke increases secretion of digestive acids, which can lead to ulcers.

Intestines: Duodenal ulcers, which are ulcers in the first length of the small intestine, can develop from the excess of stomach acid produced.

Bladder: The bladder stores and disposes of carcinogens that have been elimated from the blood. Contact with carcinogens from cigarette smoke can cause cancer.

Also affected are:

Digestive tract: Carcinogens in cigarette smoke are a potential cause of cancer in any tissue with which they come in contact, including all the components of the digestive tract—the mouth, throat, esophagus, stomach, intestines, and bladder.

Circulation: Carbon monoxide contained in cigarette smoke can affect heart functioning and even cause a heart attack. Smoking increases the risks of high blood pressure.

Female reproductive organs: Smoking increases the risk of cervical cancer in women. Pregnant women who smoke have an increased risk of miscarriage, premature birth, and infant mortality.

Smoking poses numerous health risks. Shown here are the locations of some of the most serious adverse effects of tobacco use on the body.

Did You Know That . . .

FIGURE 3.3
A Cross-section of the Lung of a Heavy Smoker

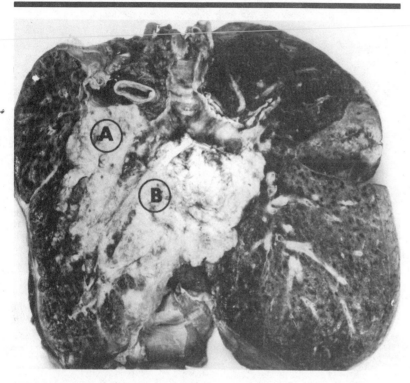

Source: American Cancer Society.

More Americans die each year as a result of smoking than were killed in all the battles of World War II and Vietnam combined.

The cancer (A) has resulted in a great narrowing of the passageway of the bronchus and the tumor has extended beyond the wall of the bronchus into the surrounding tissue (B).

malignant (cancerous) tumors. When the bronchial tree is exposed to and irritated by cigarette smoke, it produces more sputum. The smoke can also cause coughing, which in turn brings up the sputum. This extra expulsion can actually be useful during a physical examination because lung tumors are sometimes too small for an X ray to pick up but may be detected during a sputum test.

The major methods doctors use to detect lung cancer, in fact, are annual chest X rays and sputum **cytology**. Chest X rays

(continued on p. 47)

Malignant: Term used to describe a tumor which is potentially life threatening.

Cytology: The analysis of the structure of individual cells.

Chemicals in cigarette smoke will switch on a gene in lung cells that then helps make those compounds far more likely to cause cancer, researchers have reported.

The gene seems to be more likely to flick on in some people than in others, the scientists said, which may partly explain why only about 7 percent of heavy smokers develop lung cancer.

Cigarettes Trigger Lung Cancer Gene, Researchers Find

The chemicals that trigger the gene are considered the most important cancer-causing compounds in cigarette smoke and in certain environmental and industrial pollutants. As a result, the researchers said, the gene may soon be useful as a marker to identify those people who are at high risk for coming down with lung cancer.

"If we could identify those people in whom this gene is easily activated, then we could counsel them, not only not to smoke, but to avoid exposure to certain environmental pollutants," said Dr. Theodore L. McLemore, the main author of the report, in the latest issue of the *Journal of the National Cancer Institute.* Dr. McLemore, formerly a researcher at the cancer institute, now heads the pulmonary medicine division for St. Joseph's Hospital in Paris, Tex.

Quitting Usually Shuts Down Gene

He said that in normal lung tissue the gene shuts down rapidly once a person gives up smoking, becoming nearly undetectable in lung cells only two weeks later. But he and his colleagues also found that in half the lung tumors they examined the gene seemed to be stuck in a permanently active position.

"Our work supports the idea that the sooner you quit smoking, the less the chance that you'll go on to develop pulmonary cancer," Dr. McLemore said.

The gene, known as CYP1A1, normally helps liver cells tear down toxins into a harmless form that the body can easily dispose of.

But the researchers said that among those in whom the gene switches on easily, it bursts to life in the lungs when pulmonary tissue is exposed to aromatic hydrocarbons, compounds found in cigarette tar and other pollutants. The gene produces an enzyme that transforms hydrocarbons into highly reactive carcinogens that damage DNA and set the stage for cancer.

The scientists said that without the transformation resulting from the enzyme, the hydrocarbons would remain as pro-carcinogens, which cannot on their own mutate DNA.

"Unless you metabolize these pro-carcinogens of smoke into their active state, you can't have the mechanism for the production of cancer," said Dr. McLemore. "So this gene must play a very important role in the cancer cascade."

But researchers warn that even [for] those people who are shown not to have an easily triggered CYP1A1 gene, smoking is by no means risk-free. "There are about ten thousand chemicals in cigarette smoke, and this gene is involved in only one class of them," said Dr. Richard E. Kouri, director of research at BIOS Corporation in New Haven and a contributor to the research. He proposes that a number of other genes are likely to be involved in the genesis and progression of lung cancer as well.

—Natalie Angier

Source: Natalie Angier, *New York Times,* 21 August 1990, sec. 3, p. 3.

Did You Know That . . .

According to recent estimates from the National Cancer Institute, 86.1 percent of all lung cancer deaths are the result of smoking.

allow doctors to see abnormal structures in the lungs. During a cytology, the doctor examines the sputum's tissue and fluids under a microscope to detect possible abnormalities. Studies have shown that heavy smokers who receive both tests annually live longer than those who are not tested every year. [3] In addition, scientists have devised new ways of treating lung cancer; a combination of surgery and radioactive therapy has shown moderate success in prolonging the lives of some lung cancer patients. But early detection and new technology notwithstanding, the ACS reports that the 5-year survival rate for victims of lung cancer is only 5 to 8 percent. [4] It seems that the only consistent way to control this almost universally fatal disease is to avoid smoking.

Indeed, the risk of developing lung cancer is directly related to the length of time a person has smoked and the number of cigarettes he or she has consumed. A person who has been a heavy smoker for a long time is more likely to develop cancer. If and when that person quits permanently, however, his or her risk will eventually diminish until it is no different from that of a person who has never smoked. When, for example, a person who has smoked 20 cigarettes (one pack) a day for 20 years stops smoking for 10 years, that person lowers his or her risk of developing lung cancer almost to that of a nonsmoker.

Other Cancers

Although lung cancer is the most devastating and the most common of the tobacco-related cancers, it is not the only one. The ACS reports that every year 6,000 American smokers get cancer of the larynx. [5] Although this form of the disease has a relatively high survival rate—70 percent reach the 5-year mark [6]—

Over the past 3 decades, the statistical risk of dying from lung cancer has doubled for male cigarette smokers and quadrupled for female cigarette smokers.

FIGURE 3.4
Big Rise in Lung Cancer Rates

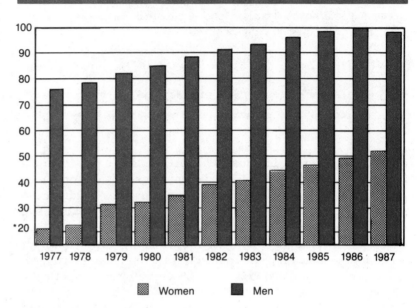

*Numbers reflect thousands of cases.
Source: American Cancer Society.

Since 1977 the national lung cancer rate for men has risen by 30 percent. The rise in lung cancer for women since 1977 is an alarming 132 percent.

many of these sufferers undergo surgical procedures to remove their larynxes and must breathe through surgically created openings in their windpipes for the rest of their lives. Often they need artificial voice boxes to help them speak. Tobacco can also contribute to the formation of cancers of the cheek, gums, lips, and tongue. Chewing tobacco is often the culprit behind these oral cancers; components in the tobacco can burn, irritate, and disintegrate mucous membranes inside the mouth, leading to the formation of malignant tumors. Cigar smoke also contains powerful irritants that can cause oral cancer, particularly that of the lips and tongue.

The American Cancer Society has implicated tobacco as a factor contributing to cancers of the esophagus, bladder, kidney, and pancreas. Smokers are 2 to 9 times as likely as nonsmokers to develop esophageal cancer, up to 7 times as likely to get urinary cancer, 1 1/2 to 2 1/2 times as likely to get kidney cancer, and 2 times as likely to develop pancreatic cancer. [7] The ACS also stresses that, as in the case of lung cancer, people who quit smoking permanently lessen their chances of getting these diseases until, after a period of time, their risk is no greater than that of a nonsmoker.

CARDIOVASCULAR DISEASE

According to the American Heart Association, cigarettes cause 120,000 deaths from heart disease every year. [8] Smokers run a higher risk than do nonsmokers of suffering **arteriosclerosis** (hardening of the arteries), which occurs when fat builds up on the blood vessel walls. In light of these dangers, the 1983 Surgeon General's Report, "Health Consequences of Smoking: Cardiovascular Disease," emphasized that cigarette smoking was the "most important of known modifiable risk factors for **coronary heart disease** in the United States." [9] The report states that as many as 30 percent of all coronary heart disease deaths are related to smoking.

The study also reaffirmed some statistics researchers had collected from a continuous study of the residents of Framingham, Massachusetts. The Framingham study examined behavior and life-style of about 5,200 residents between the ages of 30 and 62. Almost all these residents were healthy when the study began in 1948. Many have died since, but their children have become a second generation for the survey. According to the Framingham study, men and women who begin smoking at an early age, who smoke for long periods of time, and who inhale deeply run the greatest risk of developing heart disease. The study also showed a correlation between cigarette smoking and other risk factors for heart disease, such as high blood pressure and high levels of blood cholesterol.

Although epidemiological surveys such as the Framingham study show definite associations between cigarette smoking and heart disease, there has not been an overabundance of hard scientific evidence linking the two until quite recently. Scientists did know that smoking causes changes in blood chemistry and that plaque buildup can lead to heart attack and stroke, but it was not until 1986 that they discovered precisely what was responsible for this action.

That year, researchers at Cornell University Medical School

Arteriosclerosis: A group of disorders that causes thickening and loss of elasticity of artery walls.

Coronary heart disease: Temporary or permanent damage to the heart due to restricted blood flow through narrowed or blocked coronary arteries.

FIGURE 3.5
Atherosclerosis and Smoking

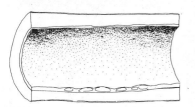

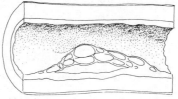

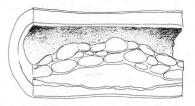

Plaque begins to form on the inner wall of an artery.

Plaque builds up and causes partial blockage of blood flow through the artery.

Further fatty deposits and plaque may cause total blockage of an artery and lead to heart attack or stroke.

Atherosclerosis occurs when fat builds up on the artery walls and restricts blood flow. Research has indicated that a chemical in tobacco smoke may stimulate this buildup and contribute to coronary heart disease.

Glycoprotein: A chemical found in tobacco smoke believed to affect the size and elasticity of arteries.

Lumen: The open space within a tubular organ, such as a vein or artery.

Angina: Heart pain caused by lack of blood flow.

Myocardial infarction: Heart attack; the sudden death of part of the heart muscle.

Apoplexy: Stroke.

Stroke: Damage to the brain caused by leakage from a ruptured blood vessel or a reduction or interruption in the blood supply.

Platelet: The smallest blood particle.

isolated a chemical in tobacco smoke called **glycoprotein**, which seemed to affect the size and elasticity of arteries.   Glycoprotein, the researchers theorized, attaches to the smooth muscular cells on the inside of the arteries and causes them to grow. Because the arteries are flexible tubes, if the cells inside them increase in size the **lumen** (hollow space inside the tube) will narrow. This action may impede blood flow to the heart, causing problems such as **angina** and **myocardial infarction**, or heart attack, which occurs when the oxygen flow to the heart is severely diminished or cut off.

Strokes

Another cardiovascular malfunction smoking can lead to is **apoplexy**, more commonly called a **stroke**. The nicotine and carbon monoxide cigarette smoke contains affect the adhesiveness of blood **platelets**, a main clotting factor in the blood. This action can harden blood vessels and form blood clots, which can flow to the brain. Such an obstruction in a cranial artery is a major cause of stroke. Nicotine can also cause blood vessels to constrict, reducing the passageways by which blood can reach the brain. When a smoker's arteries become too constricted, his or her blood supply to the brain diminishes dramatically or ceases completely, causing a stroke.

(continued on p. 52)

Did You Know That . . .

Study Says Quitting Smoking Reduces Risk of Stroke by 50%

NEW ORLEANS, Jan. 19 (AP)—Cigarette smokers who give up the habit cut their risk of stroke by about 50 percent, and even longtime smokers benefit from quitting, a new study indicates.

The findings bolster other recent research showing a strong link between smoking and stroke, the nation's third-leading cause of death. Although smoking has long been known to cause lung cancer and heart attacks, its role in promoting strokes had not [been] demonstrated until the last few years.

"There is a clear-cut relationship between cigarette smoking and stroke, and it's not too late to quit at any age," said the director of the new study, Dr. Philip A. Wolf of Boston University Medical School.

Dr. Wolf presented his data . . . at a meeting of the American Heart Association.

The study was based on 4,255 residents of Framingham, Mass., a suburb west of Boston, who took part in the long-running Framingham Heart Study. In the 26 years of the study, 459 of the participants suffered strokes.

Those who had high blood pressure were twice as likely as people with normal blood pressure to have strokes. Although smoking was not as important a risk factor as high blood pressure, the researchers found that it did increase the risk of stroke by 40 percent in men and 60 percent in women.

However, when people quit smoking, their risk of stroke fell. Two years after quitting, the former smokers' risk had decreased significantly, and after five years it was the same as that in nonsmokers.

"Whether you are a long-term smoker or a new smoker, there is even more evidence now of the benefit of stopping in terms of preserving your brain and your quality of life," said Dr. Bernadine Healy of the Cleveland Clinic Foundation.

Dr. Wolf said the link between smoking and strokes may have been missed in many earlier studies, because smokers are often thin and have lower blood pressure. This could partially protect them from strokes. However, when his analysis compared people of the same weight, there was clearly a strong association between strokes and cigarettes.

A stroke occurs when a blood vessel in the brain becomes plugged or breaks. The disease kills 152,000 people annually, making it the leading cause of death after heart attacks and cancer. . . .

If you stopped smoking 5 years ago, your risk of stroke is the same as that of a nonsmoker.

Source: *New York Times*, 19 January 1988, sec. 1, p. 16.

CHRONIC OBSTRUCTIVE LUNG DISEASES

Although the **coronary-pulmonary system** is the primary system most commonly damaged by cigarette smoking, it is by no means the only one. Another system under tobacco's siege is the respiratory system; specifically, the lungs. We have already discussed the link between tobacco and lung cancer; other diseases—often as severe—can ravage the inner workings of the lungs. **Chronic Obstructive Lung Diseases (COLD)**, such as emphysema and the more severe forms of bronchitis, account for 60,000 deaths each year and are debilitating, lifelong illnesses for thousands of people. [10]

There are thousands of people alive today with COLD. Many of them are attached to oxygen tanks, imprisoned at home or in the hospital because they are too weak to breathe on their own. Often their friends or family members will pound on their backs, temporarily freeing the lungs of the yellow mucus that impedes their breathing every day. Cigarette smoking is the only definite causal factor for COLD.

Chronic Bronchitis

Smoking-induced bronchitis results from the chronic irritation and inflammation of air passages (bronchi) leading from the windpipe to the lungs. Prolonged smoking renders a smoker's **cilia** useless; as a result, tars accumulate in the lungs. This causes a reduction in normal respiration, forcing the smoker to cough regularly and regurgitate phlegm in an attempt to expel foreign particles that his or her cilia can no longer eliminate. Bronchitis is rarely fatal, but it is an important symptom of a condition that can lead to more serious, sometimes deadly, complications.

Coronary-pulmonary system: The heart and bloodstream, and all organs and tissue related to their functioning.

Chronic obstructive lung disease (COLD): Any of a series of respiratory infections, ranging from chronic but usually harmless disorders, such as bronchitis, to potentially fatal illnesses, such as emphysema.

Cilia: Tiny hairs that line the bronchial tubes and transport mucus upwards to the throat by rhythmic wave-like actions.

Emphysema

Emphysema is a disease of the lower respiratory system. Smoking destroys the alveoli, tiny air sacs in the lungs that absorb oxygen into the body. Damage to the alveoli lessens the body's ability to absorb oxygen, so breathing becomes extremely difficult. A person with advanced emphysema may use 80 percent of his or her strength just to breathe. Advanced emphysema is extremely agonizing and usually culminates in heart failure. [11]

There is now a clear, plausible explanation of how cigarette smoking causes emphysema. The inflammatory response to cigarette smoke causes a number of cells within the smoker's lungs to become inflamed. Inflamed cells can increase the amount of elastase (an **enzyme** that acts on elastin to render it soluble) in the lung; elastase is capable of degrading elastin, one of the structural elements of the lung. In addition, cigarette smoke can block the action of elastin. The main results of all this are that

Did You Know That . . .

Smoking has been found to be the single most important cause of bronchitis and emphysema.

FIGURE 3.6
The Respiratory System

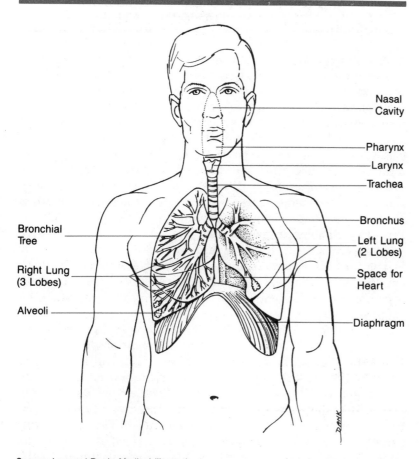

Nasal Cavity

Pharynx

Larynx

Trachea

Bronchus

Left Lung (2 Lobes)

Space for Heart

Diaphragm

Bronchial Tree

Right Lung (3 Lobes)

Alveoli

Source: Leonard Dank, Medical Illustrations.

Smoking damages the respiratory system by irritating and inflaming the bronchioles, which results in chronic bronchitis. In addition, smoking also destroys the alveoli which reduces the surface area of the lungs and can cause emphysema.

Enzyme: A protein that regulates the rate of a chemical reaction in the body.

elastase activity increases to excess, elastin in the lung diminishes, alveolar walls disappear, and emphysema develops.

Overall, the 1984 Surgeon General's Report stated the following:

> Cigarette smoking is the major cause of chronic obstructive lung disease in the United States for both men and women. The contribution of cigarette smoking to chronic obstructive lung disease morbidity and mortality far outweighs all other factors. [12]

OTHER FORMS OF TOBACCO: NO LESS DANGEROUS

"Just a pinch between the cheek and gum." Television advertisements in the 1970s and early 1980s featured a variety of athletes extolling the virtues of smokeless tobacco. They claimed that their product offered the pleasures of lit tobacco; the implication was that it was without the dangers. Such promotions were at least partially responsible for the sharp increase in the use of both chewing tobacco and snuff during that period. The truth is, however, that not just cigarettes but *all* tobacco products can cause serious, often fatal, diseases. Several studies have linked cancers of the tongue, gums, and other soft tissues of the mouth to chewing tobacco and "pinching" snuff. In light of these findings, President Ronald Reagan signed into law the Comprehensive Smokeless Tobacco Health Education Act in 1986. The new legislation outlawed radio and television advertisements for both chewing tobacco and snuff and required distributors to place warnings on smokeless tobacco containers similar to those on cigarette packages.

According to one study, "Smokeless tobacco can lead to an increase in the level of noncancerous oral conditions, particularly oral **leukoplakia** and **gingival** recession." [13] Oral leukoplakia occurs when fast-growing **lesions** form on the oral mucosa (lining of the mouth). The severity of these growths depends upon the chemical composition of the tobacco, and the growths may worsen if the sufferer continues to use the product. The illness will usually occur in three stages or degrees. During the first the gums or cheek lining will redden and become irritated. In the second stage the gums wrinkle and form valleys, and pronounced lesions appear. During the final phase fully formed lesions on the mouth's lining turn white and leathery. Approximately 5 percent of diagnosed oral leukoplakia cases turn into oral cancer.

Leukoplakia: Raised, white patches that appear on the mucous membranes lining the mouth, tongue or gums.

Gingival: Pertaining to the gums.

Lesion: A localized, abnormal, structural change in any part of the body.

(continued on p. 56)

Fighting Student Use of Smokeless Tobacco

Smokeless tobacco is easy to get and to use, and its use is growing at an alarming rate among male youths and young adults. A recent report to the Surgeon General by the Advisory Committee on the Health Consequences of Using Smokeless Tobacco concluded that smokeless tobacco products can cause oral cancer and nicotine addiction, in addition to other health consequences.

Why, then, have Americans, especially young males, chosen to risk these health problems at a time when the major form of tobacco use—cigarette smoking—is on the decline? Studies tell us that most boys are influenced to begin the use of smokeless tobacco by two powerful and related forces: peer pressure and advertising.

In a recent survey by the Department of Health and Human Services, smokeless tobacco users said the most important reason they tried the product was that their friends used it and offered it to them. Smokeless tobacco users were also much more likely than nonusers to have close friends and peers who used it. The survey also showed that dipping snuff and chewing tobacco are perceived as socially acceptable in junior and senior high schools.

Advertisements for smokeless tobacco have focused on changing the long-time image of dipping and chewing as an unattractive habit to a new image—an activity that is fun, a mark of virility, and as American as baseball and country music. In these advertisements, celebrities from major sports show how to use the product and tell how easy it is to join the ranks of heroes and role models. Thus, smokeless tobacco may be offering teenage boys an easy way to bolster a "macho" image.

Promotions of smokeless tobacco have run in print and, until the recent congressional ban on electronic advertising, on television shows that have a large young audience (such as those on competitive sports) and in adventure or sports magazines.

Advertisers also sponsor college scholarships, professional sports awards, and large-scale events such as rock or country music concerts. The events provide an opportunity for free distribution of samples, a mechanism for introducing young people to a product that they may be legally prohibited from buying.

Contests

Another marketing appeal is the "spitting contest" that producers of smokeless tobacco products hold during seasonal festivals or county fairs, often with the cosponsorship of local youth groups. Youth-oriented premiums are distributed with free samples, and prizes are awarded according to age group, including preschoolers.

The success of these advertising strategies is evident from increased use of the product as well as its association with popular youth lifestyles. For example, one popular status symbol is having a white ring on the back pocket of a pair of jeans. The ring is produced as the can of snuff stored in that pocket wears an impression into the denim.

Dipping and chewing tobacco have also become a social activity, much like cigarette smoking. In some areas, schools set aside student lounge areas for smokeless tobacco use with names like "cowboy corner," and chewing clubs for young men have sprung up.

Surveys have also shown that young people (and adults) may begin to use smokeless tobacco because they are not aware of its health consequences. Advertisements for the product have raised the invitation, "Take a pouch instead of a puff," implying a health benefit. This advertisement was withdrawn after an investigation by the attorney general of the state of New York, but the misconception remains common. Once boys begin to dip or chew, very few give up tobacco. It appears that many users progress to a more potent form of smokeless tobacco and some to cigarettes. Maintenance of the habit is not surprising, however, because the addictive potential of smokeless tobacco products appears to be at least equal to that of cigarettes. Addiction is reinforced by long, daily periods of use; some snuff users report keeping a pinch in place for 24 hours a day.

Right now, estimates of the prevalence of the use of smokeless tobacco in the United States range from about 6 million regular users to at least 12 million persons who have used some type of smokeless product in the past year. At a time when we are making substantial progress in reducing cigarette smoking, it is critical to prevent the use of smokeless tobacco from contributing to the country's leading avoidable health risk. We have the opportunity to apply to this new problem what we have learned through discouraging smoking, before the use of smokeless tobacco reaches the proportions of cigarette use.

Fortunately, many state governments and voluntary or private organizations have begun to take action. Several states require warning labels on snuff packages, levy excise taxes on smokeless tobacco products, or outlaw sales to minors (although these laws are not well known and their enforcement is weak). Some groups also conduct surveys of young users and sponsor educational programs that include printed material for students, educational packages for teachers, discussion films, etc.

Federal Effort

At the federal level, we have also begun to take key steps to reduce the use of smokeless tobacco. Legislation has been passed requiring the use of health-risk warning labels on all smokeless tobacco products and in advertisements. This legislation also prohibits advertising the products on electronic media, among other things.

We need to do more. We need more research on smokeless tobacco use among young people and on interventions to help them break this habit. But more important, we need targeted educational programs and the involvement of high school coaches, parents, athlete role models, teachers, health professionals, and young people themselves. Adoption and enforcement of restrictions on sales to young people and on advertising of smokeless tobacco products should be expanded.

Our experiences with smoking suggest that parents who abstain from or disapprove of their children's use of smokeless tobacco can have a substantial influence on their children's decision to avoid the use of smokeless tobacco. Youth heroes and role models also could be used effectively to debunk the image of smokeless tobacco.

Those who now oppose smoking should devote equal enthusiasm to discouraging the use of smokeless tobacco so we do not merely replace the ashtray with the spittoon.

—*C. Everett Koop*

Source: C. Everett Koop, *Education Digest* (December 1987), pp. 53–55.

In addition to cancer, recent research from Baylor College of Medicine and Texas Lutheran College has shown that smokeless tobacco can significantly affect the heart and blood vessels of both animals and humans. In the study, after 20 minutes of oral snuff use, the average heart rate of men younger than 20 years of age had quickened from 69 to 88 beats per minute. [14] Their average blood pressure increased from 118/72 to 126/78 during the same period.

Pipes and Cigars

People who smoke pipes and cigars instead of cigarettes reduce some hazards to their health but increase others. Because most pipe and cigar smokers do not inhale, they can more easily avoid the hot smoke filled with harmful particles and noxious gases that bombard the lung tissue and seep into the bloodstreams of cigarette smokers. As a result, they have a lower chance of developing coronary heart disease, chronic bronchitis, emphysema, or lung cancer.

People who *do* inhale when they smoke pipes and cigars increase their chances of developing serious heart and lung diseases; their chances are even higher than those of cigarette smokers. This is a special danger for former cigarette smokers. Some studies show that because they are so accustomed to inhaling, former cigarette smokers will often unintentionally continue this habit if they switch to pipes or cigars.

Even if it is not inhaled, tobacco affects the sites it touches. Hot smoke can linger inside the mouth and travel into the throat, from which it can reach the larynx (voice box) and stomach. This type of exposure, even if it is minimal, can cause cancer. In fact, the incidence of larynx and stomach cancer is frequently higher among cigar and pipe smokers than cigarette smokers. [15] And, as mentioned earlier, pipe smoking—either alone or in combination with other forms of smoking—is a direct cause of lip cancer.

Those who smoke miniature cigars face all the hazards cigarette and pipe smokers face, and, if they inhale, they risk the same consequences as cigarette smokers. Because miniature cigars are manufactured, packaged, and sold like cigarettes, people often smoke them as they would cigarettes. In addition, most brands have even higher levels of tar and nicotine than do cigarettes. For these reasons, the FTC has banned advertisements for little cigars from television and radio.

Until relatively recently, all the dire statistics concerning smoking and disease centered upon men. This was an unsurprising situation, considering that until the 1960s the number of men who smoked was far greater than that of female smokers. Women, studies showed, were happily free of lung cancer, cardiovascular disease, emphysema, and all the other insidious diseases cigarette smoking caused. Times have changed.

As the article on the next page notes, the gap between the numbers of male and female smokers is closing fast. Recent studies show that women who smoke have just as much chance of suffering smoking-related diseases as do men, as well as being susceptible to some ailments specific to their gender.

(continued on p. 60)

Did You Know That . . .

Thomas Edison, who loved cigars, refused to employ cigarette smokers.

Women and Tobacco

When smoking amongst women was not as widespread as it is now, women were considered to be almost free from cardiovascular diseases and lung cancer. Unhappily, the situation has changed, and smoking kills over half a million women each year in the industrialised world. But it is also an increasingly important cause of ill-health amongst women in developing countries.

A recent WHO Consultation on the statistical aspects of tobacco-related mortality concluded that the toll that can be attributed to smoking throughout the world is 2.7 million deaths per year. It also predicted that, if current patterns of cigarette smoking continue unchanged, the global death toll from tobacco by the year 2025 may increase to eight million deaths per year. A large proportion of these will be amongst women.

Despite these alarming statistics, the scale of the threat that smoking poses to women's health has received surprisingly little attention. Smoking is still seen by many as a mainly male problem, perhaps because men were the first to take up the habit and therefore the first to suffer the ill-effects. This is no longer the case. Women who smoke like men will die like men. WHO estimates that, in industrialised countries, smoking rates amongst men and women are very similar, at around 30 per cent; in a large number of developed countries, smoking is now more common among teenage girls than boys. In most developing countries, where it is generally estimated that 50 per cent of men and five per cent of women smoke, the epidemic seems not to have reached women yet. But as cigarettes become more widely available and more heavily promoted, trends are changing.

As women took up smoking later than men, the full impact of smoking on their health has yet to be seen. But it is clear from countries where women have smoked longest, such as the United Kingdom and the United States, that smoking causes the same diseases in women as in men and the gap between their death rates is narrowing. On current trends, some 20 to 25 per cent of women who smoke will die from their habit. One in three of these deaths will be among women under 65 years of age. The US Surgeon General has estimated that, amongst these women, smoking is responsible for around 40 per cent of heart disease deaths, 55 per cent of lethal strokes and, among women of all ages, 80 per cent of lung cancer deaths and 30 per cent of all cancer deaths. Over the last 20 years, death rates in women from lung cancer have more than doubled in Japan, Norway, Poland, Sweden and the United Kingdom; have increased by more than 200 per cent in Australia, Denmark and New Zealand; and have increased by more than 300 per cent in Canada and the United States.

There are dramatically increasing trends in respiratory cancer among women in developed countries, and the causal relationship of smoking, rather than air pollution and other factors, to lung cancer is very clear. In the United States, for instance, the mortality rate for lung cancer among female non-smokers has not changed during the past 20 years. During the same period, the rate among female smokers has increased by a factor of five. Smoking is already an important cause of cancer in many developing countries. In South-East Asia, more than 85 per cent of oral cancer cases in women are caused by tobacco habits.

Smoking also affects women's health in ways that are specific to women, and that put them at added risk. Women smokers have higher rates of cervical cancer, while those who smoke and use the oral contraceptive pill are several times more likely to develop cardiovascular diseases than those who use neither. Smoking affects women's reproductive health, increasing the risks of earlier menopause, miscarriage and low birthweight babies—a major concern in those developing countries where a baby's health is already jeopardised by poverty and malnutrition. Smokers are more prone to osteoporosis, a major cause of fractures in older people, particularly post-menopause women.

Women's health is also affected by the smoking of others, that is, by passive or involuntary smoking; for example, it has been shown that non-smoking wives of heavy smokers run a higher risk of lung cancer. In addition to these direct effects, we should not forget the indirect ones such as the additional burden in economic and non-economic terms that must be carried mainly by the mother as a consequence of morbidity and mortality of other family members from tobacco-associated diseases.

Protection, education, support

What can be done to halt and reverse the tobacco epidemic amongst women? The challenge is twofold: to reduce the already high level of smoking among women in the industrialised world and to ensure that the low level of smoking in developing countries does not increase. In order to achieve these goals, all countries need to develop comprehensive anti-tobacco programmes which take into account and address the needs of women. Whilst these programmes should be culture-specific and tailored to meet the local situation, experts agree that to be successful they must contain three key elements: protection, education and support.

Young girls and women need to be protected from inducements to smoke. Tobacco is a multi-national, multi-billion dollar industry. It is also an industry under threat; one quarter of its customers, in the long-term, are killed by using its product and smoking is declining in many industrialised countries. To maintain profits, tobacco companies need to ensure that at least 2.7 million new smokers, usually young people, start smoking every year. Women have been clearly identified as a key target group for tobacco advertising in both the industrialised and developing worlds. Billions of US dollars each year are spent on promoting this lethal product specifically to women. "Women only" brands, widespread advertisements depicting beautiful, glamorous, successful women smoking, free fashion goods, and the sponsorship of women's sports and events (such as tennis and fashion shows), are all part of the industry's global marketing strategy aimed at attracting and keeping women smoking.

This strategy has been highlighted by several tobacco journals which have carried articles on "Targeting the female smoker" and suggesting that retailers should "look to the ladies". Among the 20 US magazines that received the most cigarette advertising revenue in 1985, eight were women's magazines. In the same year, a study on the cigarette advertising policies of 53 British women's magazines (read by more than half of all British women) showed that 64 per cent of the magazines accepted cigarette advertising, which represented an average of seven per cent of total advertising revenue.

Research in industrialised countries has shown the subtle methods used to encourage young girls to smoke. The impact of such methods is likely to be even greater in developing countries, where young people are generally less knowledgeable about smoking hazards and may be more attracted by glamorous, affluent, desirable images of the female smoker. This is why WHO, together with other national and international health agencies, has repeatedly called for national legislation banning all forms of tobacco promotion, and for an appropriate "high price" policy which would slow down the "enthusiasm" of young women for tobacco consumption.

Resisting the pressures

Young girls and women have a right to be informed about the damage that smoking can do to their health. They also need to acquire skills to resist pressures to start smoking or to give it up. Several countries have developed integrated school and pre-school health education programmes which have successfully reduced girls' smoking rates; but this education should not be restricted to what happens in school. There are many other examples of effective cessation programmes in the workplace and primary health centres. Unfortunately, many women do not have the opportunity to be involved in such programmes, and programmes have generally been less successful with women than men. In countries where smoking has decreased, the rate of decline has been usually lower in women than men, and least amongst women with low education and income. This suggests that educational initiatives ought to be more sensitive to women's needs; they also ought to cover issues of particular significance to women—such as the gain in weight that sometimes occurs after they stop smoking.

They need support

In order for women to become, and remain, non-smokers they need support. Support over these difficult days when the addiction cycle is broken. Support to help them deal in other less damaging ways with the reasons that caused them to smoke. Many women use smoking as a coping strategy, for example to create a "space" in a day filled with the stress of bringing up children and having to face different types of work, often with little social support and on a low income. Environments need to be created which enable them to break free of this health-damaging behaviour, to make the healthy choices the best choices.

Smoking amongst women has already reached epidemic proportions and will continue to escalate unless action is taken now. Delays can only cause further suffering and deaths of women; this is why WHO's new programme on Tobacco or Health is giving high priority to action to protect women and children.

But what can be done to tackle this problem? Community health workers can develop health education programmes for young girls. Primary care workers can ensure that all women receive information, advice and support to help them give up the habit. Governments, national and international non-governmental organizations, and WHO in particular, can act as advocates for women's health to ensure that the issue of women and tobacco is put high on the health and political agenda, by pressing for action to protect women. Strategies to this effect should involve health and educational services, community and women's organizations, the media and even the employers.

Only by exposing the previously hidden problem of women and tobacco, only by putting women in the picture, will we be able to secure major improvements in the health of women worldwide.

—Amanda Amos and
Claire Chollat-Traquet

Source: Amanda Amos and Claire Chollat-Traquet, "Women Who Smoke," *World Health* (April–May 1990), pp. 7–8.

CONCLUDING REMARKS

This chapter has examined many of tobacco's hazardous effects on the human body. Smokers take their lives into their own hands every time they light a cigarette, for the damages they subject themselves to can be deadly. But the risks smokers run are only part of the story; tobacco can harm nonsmokers as well. The unborn children of women who smoke and bystanders who work or live with heavy smokers can suffer severe internal damage, leading to uncomfortable, often debilitating diseases or defects. They are innocent victims, the subjects of the next chapter. ⟨W⟩

The Innocent Victims

ANY ARGUMENT that supports a person's right to engage in something potentially dangerous relies strongly on the notion that the chosen activity— whether it's race car driving, fire swallowing, or walking a tightrope—will harm only the participant and not innocent passersby. For many years, advocates of smokers' rights applied this theory in good faith, believing that only smokers themselves could suffer lung cancer, bronchitis, or any of the other diseases caused by cigarettes. There was, they stressed, no documented proof to the contrary, but in late 1986 two reports delivered a stunning blow to these advocates. In their respective reports, both the National Research Council and the U.S. Surgeon General found that **environmental smoke**—that is, sidestream smoke from a cigarette (see chapter 3)—could threaten the health of nonsmokers who are exposed to it. In the meantime, scientists were gathering increasing evidence linking smoking during pregnancy to such birth defects as **low birth weight**. By the end of 1986, the message was clear: Smoking is dangerous not only to those who smoke, but to nonsmokers and unborn children as well.

SOME STARTLING RESULTS

The two 1986 reports were both based on comprehensive studies and reached very similar conclusions. For the sake of simplicity, this book will focus mostly on the first of the two studies to be released, that of the National Research Council. This report examined the amount of chemicals passive smokers inhale and

(continued on p. 63)

Environmental smoke: Cigarette smoke released directly into the air and sometimes inhaled by nearby nonsmokers; sidestream smoke.

Low birth weight: An abnormally underweight measurement for newborn babies; may result from smoking during pregnancy.

[In 1964] the Surgeon General's Advisory Committee on Smoking and Health released its landmark report and revealed to the American public irrefutable evidence that smoking is a deadly habit. Since then there has been dramatic change in public knowledge, attitudes and behavior.

Nearly half the adults alive who ever smoked have quit. The

Involuntary Smoking Increases Health Risks of Spouses and Children

prevalence of smoking has fallen from 40% in 1965 to 29% in 1987. It is becoming less and less socially acceptable to smoke, and restrictions on smoking in public places are increasing. Nevertheless, smoking remains one of the most important preventable causes of death in Americans. More than one in every six deaths is attributable to smoking.

Thanks to years of public education, nearly all smokers know the habit is "hazardous to their health." Now increasing attention is being given to the effects of involuntary or passive smoking.

What is involuntary smoking?

Involuntary smoking is the inhalation of tobacco smoke by non-smokers when they are in enclosed environments with smokers. "Mainstream smoke" is the smoke exhaled into the room by the smoker. "Sidestream smoke" is the smoke emitted directly into the surrounding air from the lit end of the cigarette. Both types of smoke contain nicotine, carbon monoxide and various chemical irritants and cancer-causing agents.

Spouses of smokers have increased risk of lung cancer

Studies have shown that non-smokers married to smokers have an increased risk of lung cancer of 20 to 50% or more. The risk increases with the amount the spouse smokes. It was recently estimated that 4,700 lung cancer deaths per year among non-smokers can be attributed to passive smoking.

Young children are especially at risk

Pregnant women are routinely warned of the serious risks their smoking presents to their unborn children. Though a large number of them stop smoking during pregnancy, many start again after the child is born. What they may not know, however, is that parental smoking—and especially maternal smoking—also presents risks to infants and young children.

Numerous studies in the United States and abroad have demonstrated that there is a dramatic increase in the risk of respiratory illness for the young children of smoking parents. For example, one British study showed a 32% increase in bronchitis and pneumonia in the first year of life when mothers smoked. In Washington, D.C., 89% more infants whose parents smoked were found to have **tracheitis**, and 44% more young children developed bronchitis. Another study, which took a random sample of children under age 5, found that children of smoking mothers have almost twice the risk of acute upper respiratory tract infection than children of non-smoking mothers.

Furthermore, it has been estimated that 10% to 35% of all chronic middle ear effusions in children could be attributable to smoking exposure. Again, this has been substantiated by many studies.

In short, it has consistently been found that young children are particularly vulnerable to the effects of involuntary smoke. They have an increased risk of a variety of acute respiratory illnesses including tracheitis, bronchitis and pneumonia, as well as an increase in the incidence of middle ear disease. The figures also seem to indicate that mothers' smoking is a more significant factor than fathers' smoking.

Final comment

Active smoking remains a major public health problem; however, involuntary smoking is clearly a problem that deserves serious attention. Adults may have some choice about their exposure, but children do not. Since approximately 70% of children in the United States live in homes where there is at least one adult smoker, their great vulnerability to the effects of involuntary smoking is a cause of serious concern.

—Alan Gross, M.D.

Source: Alan Gross, *News and Health Bulletin*, Vol. 8, No. 6 (November 1989), p. 4.

Did You Know That . . .

Children who are regularly exposed to secondhand tobacco smoke suffer more frequent and more severe respiratory infections than do children of nonsmokers.

found that nonsmokers exposed to sidestream smoke (also called environmental tobacco smoke, or ETS) had significantly higher levels of nicotine in their blood, urine, and saliva than those who were not exposed. [1]

Next the report looked at how passive smoking among pregnant women affected the growth of their newborns. Later on in this chapter we will take a look at the damages pregnant women who smoke cause their unborn children. Husbands who smoke and expose their pregnant wives who do not smoke to ETS may also cause damage. One study, first done in 1966 and confirmed in 1971, found that babies of mothers exposed to ETS from a smoking father suffer almost as high an incidence of low birth weight as do the babies of actively smoking mothers. [2] Furthermore, the study found that the low birth weight babies of actively smoking mothers were in fact healthier than those of actively

Tracheitis: Inflammation of the windpipe or trachea.

smoking fathers (and, therefore, passively smoking mothers). [3] Another study of 5,000 children done in 1973 showed that babies whose fathers smoked more than 10 cigarettes a day had a higher incidence of **prenatal death** than did the babies of nonsmoking parents. [4] Finally, the most recent study, conducted in 1986 among 500 newborn babies, found that smoking among fathers during the first trimester of the mothers' pregnancy reduced the weight of their newborn babies 12 grams (about half an ounce) per 10 cigarettes smoked per day. [5] In other words, if the husband of a pregnant woman smokes a pack each day—and his wife is exposed to the sidestream smoke of each cigarette—that baby's weight will be reduced by one ounce each day.

The dangers of passive smoking do not end for a child once he or she is born. One study found that children exposed to ETS at home on a regular basis had a lower rate of growth than did children of nonsmoking parents; more specifically, the children studied lost .03 cms a day from their normal rate of growth for every 20 cigarettes smoked each day in their home. [6] Three surveys of the children over the age of 5 who had smoking mothers (including those whose mothers did not smoke during pregnancy) found that the exposure to sidestream smoke curtailed the development of the children's lung capacity. That is, the growth of each child's lung capacity was much slower and less complete than that of the children of nonsmoking mothers.

Possibly related to this finding are the studies citing the rate of lung irritation suffered by children of smoking parents. Six studies in the report found that this group suffered a significantly higher incidence of minor lung infections, such as wheezing and coughing, than do the children of nonsmoking parents. One such study, which surveyed 5,000 British students who live at home, found that while 16 percent of children with nonsmoking parents had a cough, 18 percent of children with one smoking parent had a cough, and 23.5 percent of children with two smoking parents suffered this irritation. [7] Other studies showed that bronchitis and **pneumonia** occurred more frequently in children with one or more smoking parents than in those whose parents did not smoke. Yet another study found a direct relationship between the amount of maternal smoking and the rate of lung infection during the first year of life. [8] This relationship lessened significantly during the second year of life and disappeared altogether during the third.

Just as shocking as the statistics concerning children were the report's findings involving the link between passive smoking and lung cancer. The findings published in the report concerned

Prenatal death: Death before birth.

Pneumonia: Inflammation of the lungs, caused by viral or bacterial infection.

(continued on p. 66)

Higher Risk Is Found Among Children of Smokers

For the first time, researchers have shown that nonsmoking adults who grew up in households with smokers have an increased risk of lung cancer.

Although 83 percent of all lung cancer occurs among cigarette smokers, the researchers said their findings suggest that 17 percent of the cases among nonsmokers result from secondhand tobacco smoke they breathed at home as children.

The finding . . . adds to the evidence that secondhand smoke is a health hazard. It had earlier been linked to heart disease, respiratory problems in children and lung cancer in the spouses of smokers.

Based on its own analysis of lung cancer in women who had never smoked, the Federal Environmental Protection Agency . . . listed secondhand smoke as a known human carcinogen. Steven Bayard, a statistician for the E.P.A., said the agency would try to use data from the new study in further assessing the risks of secondhand smoke.

Doubled Risk of Cancer

The study . . . involved almost 400 people throughout upstate New York. It found that the risk of lung cancer was about double the usual one for nonsmokers.

The study also found no statistically significant increase in lung cancer risk from exposure to smoke from a spouse or from colleagues in a workplace. But the researchers said they were not sure that the study was precise enough to spot any such increased risk.

The estimate from the study suggests that 1,700 cases of lung cancer each year result from childhood exposure to secondhand smoke, according to figures from the E.P.A. The agency said that of the 150,000 new cases of lung cancer diagnosed each year, about 25,000 involve people who are not currently smokers and about 10,000 who never smoked.

The study is based on a 1987 doctoral thesis that a Yale physician, Dr. Luis R. Varela, prepared before his death [in 1990]. The report was written by Dr. Dwight T. Janerich, who started the study when he worked for the New York State Department of Health, and eight colleagues from the National Cancer Institute, Memorial Sloan-Kettering Cancer Center in New York, Albany Medical College and the University of Southern Maine.

The tobacco industry has challenged the environmental agency's position on secondhand smoke. Officials of the Philip Morris Companies had widely distributed Dr. Varela's thesis, which found no increased cancer risk from exposure to smoke from a spouse or from co-workers, to advance its case that secondhand smoke was not as dangerous as the environmental agency and a number of leading medical researchers have reported.

Steven C. Parrish, a vice president of Philip Morris, said . . . that the new findings about the dangers to children "are worth looking at in further research" into occupations and other possible environmental hazards. But Mr. Parrish called the new findings "consistent with our view that there is no increased risk to spouses and in the workplace.". . .

Studies Differ on Spousal Smoking

Epidemiologists have commonly used a spouse's smoking habits to measure the risk of secondhand smoke. Overall statistical analyses of a collection of studies of secondhand smoking have found an increased risk of cancer, even when including studies that individually showed no detectable rise in risk.

Dr. Janerich said, "We certainly did not find evidence to reject the findings in the earlier studies."

He said it is possible that physical circumstances and differences in study areas, the size of residences, ventilation, and other important physical aspects of the living conditions, as well as social habits that affect exposure within the family, will need to be measured and analyzed before the differences in findings among the studies can be reconciled.

Dr. Janerich said he did not know how his team's data would change the evidence for the dangers of secondhand smoking if the environmental agency carried out a new overall statistical analysis.

Effect on Child's Lungs

Dr. Janerich's team studied 191 patients who had been diagnosed with lung cancer from 1982 through 1984. The patients had either never smoked more than 100 cigarettes or had smoked at one time but not more than 100 cigarettes in the 10 years before the diagnosis of cancer. The group was compared with an equal number of people without lung cancer who had never smoked.

The researchers added up the number of years that each person lived in a house and multiplied it by the number of smokers to calculate smoker years. The researchers found that household exposure of 25 or more smoker years

during childhood and adolescence doubled the risk of lung cancer.

The risk of lung cancer did not appear to increase with household exposure during adult life. Dr. Janerich said that the higher rates from childhood exposures could be because lung cancer takes many years to develop.

Dr. Janerich urged that animal studies be made to determine whether a growing lung was more susceptible to the initiation of cancer. He also urged researchers conducting new studies to measure the amount of smoke in the workplace to get a better grasp of the hazards of different amounts of cigarette smoke.

Dr. Janerich said the study was begun in 1980 to determine what percentage of lung cancers in nonsmokers was due to smoking and was not intended to be a study of all hazards of secondhand smoking.

—*Lawrence K. Altman*

Source: Lawrence K. Altman, *New York Times*, 12 September 1990, sec. 2, p. 12.

nonsmokers married to smokers. According to these findings, exposure to sidestream smoke increases the lung cancer risk of a person married to a smoker by 25 percent. [9] The same studies reported that nonsmokers who are not married to smokers but who may come in regular contact with ETS in the workplace or in a restaurant have an 8 percent increased risk of getting the disease compared to those who are not exposed at all. All in all, the National Academy of Sciences reports that passive smoking may be responsible for as many as 24,000 deaths from lung cancer every year. [10] The report's final conclusion is that passive smokers receive about 3/4 of 1 percent of the elements active smokers inhale, and that for every 100,000 people exposed to ETS, 390 will suffer lung cancer.

Published a month after the first report, the 1986 Surgeon General's Report reached the same conclusions: Passive smoking can cause disease in nonsmokers, and children of parents who smoke have a greater risk of suffering respiratory infections such

(continued on p. 68)

There's no denying that cigarettes are a lethal addiction: smoking kills more than six times as many Americans every year as died in the entire Vietnam War. But *secondhand* smoke remains a source of bitter contention. Is it really a public-health hazard, as the antismoking forces contend? Or is it just an annoyance? [In 1986], the U.S. Surgeon General's office and the National Research Council tackled the question. In separate reports, both firmly linked passive smoking to lung cancer. They also found that smokers' children suffered more than their share of respiratory infections. But neither panel tried to gauge the overall impact of passive smoking on the nation's health. The evidence was still too sketchy.

Secondhand Smoke: Some Grim News

That was [in 1986]. . . . In a draft report [released in 1990], the EPA [has concluded] that secondhand smoke causes 3,800 lung-cancer deaths in the United States every year. . . . The second new study, by San Francisco heart researcher Stanton Glantz, suggests that lung cancer is only the beginning of the problem. Indeed, Glantz calculates that passive smoking causes 10 times as much heart disease as lung disease, making it the nation's third leading cause of preventable death. The only bigger killers, he says, are active smoking and alcohol abuse.

The new EPA report—based on results from 24 epidemiological studies, including 11 that weren't on hand in 1986—could carry a lot of political weight. An accompanying "guide to workplace smoking policies" will recommend that employers create separately ventilated smoking lounges, since segregation alone offers nonsmokers little protection. The EPA doesn't regulate cigarette smoke, but declaring it a known hazard could make way for tough local smoking ordinances. Already, Los Angeles City Councilman Marvin Braude has proposed an outright ban on smoking in restaurants, saying the new studies take us "way beyond the days when restaurant smoking laws were introduced just to make dining a more pleasurable experience."

The Philip Morris company, a staunch opponent of such restrictions, has launched a pre-emptive strike against the EPA report but has succeeded mainly at drawing attention to it. In a press release, the firm implie[d] that the EPA [was] neglecting a Yale University study that tends to exonerate passive smoking. Though that study, an unpublished 1987 Ph.D. dissertation, suggested that previous research may have overestimated the danger, it actually supported "the existence of a small-to-moderate effect of passive smoking on lung-cancer risks." And as Philip Morris concedes, the results were not in a form that could be integrated into the EPA's data pool.

The dissertation relied on data from a research project run by Yale epidemiologist Dwight Janerich, but it wasn't the last word on the project. In a new paper, summarized in the printed program of a recent

Did You Know That . . .

Passive smokers are up to 3 times more likely to die from lung cancer than those who are not regularly exposed to secondhand smoke.

cancer conference, Janerich reported that the risk of lung cancer nearly doubled in subjects who were exposed to a given quantity of secondhand smoke during early life. By estimating the number of people so exposed and applying the risk factor, Janerich deduced that passive smoking may be responsible for 20 percent of all lung cancer in nonsmokers. That's a slightly *higher* estimate than the EPA came up with. Philip Morris spokesman Thomas Borelli speculates that Janerich "tortured the data" until it said what he wanted to hear.

Heart disease: Lung cancer aside, the accumulating evidence on heart disease should give the industry pause. By pooling and analyzing the results of 11 recent studies, Stanton Glantz and his collaborator, Dr. William Parmley, showed that living with a smoker has roughly the same effect on heart-disease mortality that it has on lung-cancer mortality: both rise by about 30 percent in the nonsmoker. But because heart disease is 10 times as prevalent as lung cancer, the same risk factor yields 30,000 to 40,000 annual deaths. Combining that toll with 3,000 to 4,000 lung-cancer deaths, and factoring in an estimated 10,000 deaths from nonlung cancers caused by passive smoking, Glantz gets a grand total of about 50,000 deaths. In short, one nonsmoker dies for every eight smokers.

Glantz is not the first scientist to reach this startling conclusion; another researcher, Judson Wells, published similar figures in 1988. But Glantz's paper is the most comprehensive review to date, and it goes beyond epidemiology to describe the mechanisms by which secondhand smoke might affect the heart. Viewed as a whole, he says, "the evidence on heart disease is stronger today than the evidence on lung cancer was in 1986." One shudders to think what the next round of studies will show.

—Geoffrey Cowley

Source: Geoffrey Cowley, *Newsweek* (11 June 1990), p. 59.

as bronchitis and pneumonia than do children of nonsmoking parents. [11] Furthermore, the report stressed that the risk of passive smoking would not be eliminated by separating nonsmokers and smokers within the same air space.

NONSMOKERS VS. SMOKERS

The excitement and passionate responses the publication of the two reports generated was not limited to nonsmokers. Representatives from the tobacco companies protested the studies' conclusions, claiming that the findings were not conclusive. This may be true to a certain extent. It is very difficult to establish beyond

(continued on p. 72)

Tobacco Science Wars

The debate over cigarettes and public health broke new ground with the release [in 1986] of two reports on the danger tobacco poses for nonsmokers. The National Academy of Sciences (NAS) and the U.S. Surgeon General found that exposure to other people's cigarette smoke may have lethal consequences. The tobacco industry has reacted strongly, attacking not only this information, but the scientists behind it.

In a [1987] interview, two outspoken scientists, James Repace of the Environmental Protection Agency (EPA) and Stanton A. Glantz of the University of California at San Francisco, accused the tobacco industry of grossly misusing scientific data. The propaganda war has grown ugly, they say, and in order to feed it, the industry has used the work of its consultants to denigrate sound research and confuse the public.

Industry representatives, meanwhile, say their experts have been harassed by antismoking "zealots" and that their right to free expression has been infringed.

According to Repace and Glantz, the industry faces a crisis because new data link environmental tobacco smoke with lung cancer and other chronic diseases. Industry consultants—for example, Sorell L. Schwartz of Georgetown University—concede that smokers get lung cancer and that children of smoking mothers are more likely to have respiratory problems. But they have focused their considerable intelligence on refuting a much narrower point: the case that environmental smoke causes lung cancer in nonsmokers. For the industry, the objective may be to forestall prohibitions on smoking in the workplace.

Over a dozen epidemiological studies, some strong, some weak, have found an association between exposure to smoke and an increased risk of lung cancer in nonsmokers. One problem in them is that nearly all rely on marriage as the link. Women married to smokers are considered the high-risk "exposed" group, and are compared with "unexposed" wives of nonsmokers.

The spouses of smokers have about a 30% greater risk of getting lung cancer, according to the National Academy of Sciences report.

One potential weakness of this approach is that people tend to have the same smoking habits as their spouses, regardless of what they tell researchers, and "never-smokers," in fact, may be ex-smokers. This tendency to misclassify may explain why the spouses of smokers are more likely to get cancer. But a careful analysis of the epidemiological research, conducted by Nicholas Wald of St. Bartholomew's Hospital, London, for the NAS, found in all the studies a "highly significant association" between lung cancer and exposure to environmental tobacco smoke, a result too great to be explained by systematic bias. The NAS concluded that there is a cause-and-effect relationship.

The number of nonsmokers who die each year may be perhaps several thousand, small compared with 350,000 deaths caused by direct smoking. But public health problems smaller than this have prompted government action. A huge bureaucracy now regulates pesticides, food additives, and airborne chemicals. The question arises: why not control tobacco smoke? The tobacco industry worries that this kind of reasoning may lead to a ban on smoking indoors. At a minimum, it may lead to a quarantine of smokers.

Repace, a physicist who runs the technical services office for EPA's indoor air program, wrote some early influential papers linking ambient smoke and cancer, most of them on his own time. Glantz, an associate professor of medicine, has published a biostatistics textbook and is chairman of the UCSF graduate program in bioengineering. Both regard cigarette smoke as a toxic pollutant that should be kept out of public places.

The Tobacco Institute, the industry's arm in Washington, claims it is "anti-smoking activists" who are guilty of abusing the scientific process. The Institute made such charges in a 53-page booklet in December 1986 ("Tobacco Smoke and the Nonsmoker: Scientific Integrity at the Cross-roads"). It says, among other things, that anti-smoking advocates forced a scientific workshop at Georgetown University to be cancelled last year because it was sponsored by industry.

Repace responded in an interview by laying out his own version of the propaganda war. As he began, he was hit unexpectedly with what he calls "the most powerful threat that can be made against a government employee." On 12 March [1987], Representative Don Sundquist (R-TN) sent a letter to the head of EPA, Lee Thomas, denouncing Repace for personal misconduct.

Sundquist was not available to comment. His aide, Thomas McNamara, said this was an old matter that had been "percolating" for about 2 years, ever since Sundquist had been involved in a study of passive smoking by the Office of Technology Assessment. Echoing an industry complaint, Sundquist said he found Repace's study confusing because it was the work of an EPA scientist, but had no official EPA backing. In response, Repace says he always attaches a disclaimer to his papers to make it clear that he does not speak for the agency.

Sundquist alleges that Repace has violated EPA's code of ethics by serving for pay (while on leave) as a witness in labor grievance hearings and trials for people with smoking complaints. He has also testified as a citizen in favor of controls on smoking. This career, according to Sundquist, conflicts with Repace's public role because it makes him unable to give a fair hearing to the tobacco company side.

Repace denies this, saying he is always open to new scientific information, and has received advance clearance for each case of off-hours testimony. He was shaken by the letter, however, because it has triggered a full-scale ethics inquiry. He says, "I now face a protracted investigation. Even if I am fully exonerated, it will give my supervisors extra work. They may ask, 'Do we really want someone who causes this kind of trouble?' " The information on fees in Sundquist's letter, according to Repace, is highly detailed, the kind a detective might dig up. "I wonder where he got it."

According to McNamara, "We asked around

town who this guy was, and obviously we asked the tobacco industry. They provided us with this information, which we sent to the administrator" of EPA.

Repace says this is the latest of many examples of industry meddling in the scientific debate. He claims to know of other cases in which industry consultants have lobbied against papers about to be published in scientific journals. He also mentions a Japanese scientist, Takeshi Hirayama, who reported in 1981 that nonsmoking wives of smokers in Japan were twice as likely to get lung cancer as wives of nonsmokers. Suddenly he found his research attacked not just in letters to the *British Medical Journal,* but in full-page magazine and newspaper ads all across the United States. Scientists are capable of dealing with substantive criticism, Repace says, but not multimillion-dollar ad campaigns.

Repace's own work was the target of a tobacco industry blast in May 1985 ("Situation Report: Tobacco Smoke in the Air"). Of Repace, it said, "He can hardly be described as a qualified authority," because he is merely a physicist, not a physician. It attacked several weak points in his study, points that Repace says he dealt with in the text of the paper. One issue was Repace's use of a group of Seventh Day Adventists for his "control" group of nonsmokers. Critics point out that the Seventh Day Adventists use a diet loaded with green and yellow vegetables, which are thought to aid in the prevention of cancer. Repace cited other research indicating that the Adventists' healthy diet is not enough to account for the entire reduction in risk, and, in any case, that it would be offset by exposure to smoke in offices where some of them work.

The industry report stressed an ad hominem approach, calling Repace and other researchers "long-time, highly vocal antismoking activists." On this point, Repace finds himself in good company. Surgeon General C. Everett Koop, who would like to create a "smokeless society" in the United States, also has been attacked many times in harsh terms.

It was about a year after publication of this pamphlet that Repace wrote a memo for the American Lung Association that truly incensed the Tobacco Institute. Repace focused on the testimony of Philip Witorsch, a pulmonary specialist at George Washington University, who had traveled at industry expense to municipal hearings around the country to point out flaws in Repace's work. The memo, distributed by the Lung Association, says that tobacco industry consultants are "notable for their lack of expertise" and should be viewed as "paid advocates who receive hefty consultant fees to defend an industry from potential economic losses."

More insidious than the challenge to individuals, says Glantz, are the attempts to jam the scientific airwaves with noise. Glantz quotes from a cigarette company (Brown and Williamson) document subpoenaed by the Federal Trade Commission in 1969. He says it lays out a public relations strategy still used by the industry:

> Doubt is our product since it is the best means of competing with the 'body of fact' that exists in the mind of the general public. It is also the means of establishing a controversy. If we are successful at establishing a controversy at the public level, then there is an opportunity to put across the real facts about smoking and health.

One industry method of fomenting doubt, according to Glantz, is to run scientific meetings to which well-established researchers and industry consultants are invited as speakers. The consultants voice doubts about other people's research, and the doubts are repeated in letters to the editor and advertisements in the popular media.

There have been several skirmishes over the propriety of such conferences in recent years. The bitterest broke out last summer at Georgetown University. Sorell Schwartz, a Georgetown pharmacologist and tobacco industry consultant, put together a group of experts for the industry called the "Indoor Air Pollution Advisory Group" in the spring of 1985. Its members, all academics, have been flown around the country by the tobacco industry to speak about the weakness of the data on environmental tobacco smoke.

"We decided we should have a seminar on the science of environmental tobacco smoke," Schwartz says, and he arranged to hold it at Georgetown in June 1986. With the help of the Tobacco Institute, he secured funding from two tobacco companies and other sponsors. Included among the speakers were several authors of the National Academy of Sciences and U.S. Surgeon General's reports on passive smoking, then being written. Most of the moderators were members of Schwartz's industry consulting team.

Through inadvertence, Schwartz says, he failed to have an assistant notify speakers that the conference was sponsored in part by cigarette companies. For other technical reasons, he also failed to print this information in the program. To critics, it looked as though the industry was trying to undermine the upcoming scientific reports. As one person said, "I was worried about seeing my name in an R. J. Reynolds ad," printed under a summary written by an industry consultant. Another invitee found it "deceptive" that the invitation came from Georgetown University and not directly from the tobacco consulting group.

The American Lung Association protested vehemently and asked Georgetown to cancel the meeting. Donald R. Shopland, acting director of the surgeon general's office of smoking and health, told his authors about the event's sponsorship and warned them to be careful about what they said in public. Three speakers withdrew. F. Charles Hiller of the University of Arkansas Medical School wrote Schwartz a strong letter saying he would not have come had he known of the extent of tobacco company involvement. Another invitee, Anna H. T. Wu of the University of Southern California, withdrew because she had not been told about the sponsors. The third, A. Sonia Buist of the Oregon Health Sciences University in Portland, withdrew citing a scheduling conflict. All say they were not pressured.

Georgetown did not yield to the Lung Association, but Schwartz decided to cancel "on my own." He says, "I was dealing in an area I'd never dealt with before—solid emotion—and I didn't feel comfortable."

In its latest pamphlet, the Tobacco Institute

describes all this as "a direct threat to scientific integrity" and an "attempt to stifle free speech and academic freedom." It gives other examples of harassment by the "forces dedicated to the prohibition of cigarette smoking." For example, the Institute says "a tenured professor at a major state university was threatened with the loss of research funds by the state's health commissioner, but had the strength to assert his right to speak the truth." The professor in question, Salvatore R. DiNardi of the University of Massachusetts at Amherst, is a consultant in Schwartz's industry group. According to his department chairman, Gary S. Moore, he drew fire from alumni and comment from the dean for his testimony on behalf of the tobacco industry. But Moore says he was never in danger of losing research support.

Meanwhile, according to Shopland, the Tobacco Institute has come after him. Two letters addressed to the Secretary of Health and Human Services, Otis Bowen, seek an investigation into the surgeon general's and Shopland's alleged misconduct. The president of the Tobacco Institute demands a personal meeting with Bowen.

It is hard to say whether tactics like this will help or hinder the tobacco industry's cause. But if Glantz is correct that the industry likes to sow controversy, then it is reaping a rich harvest.

—*Eliot Marshall*

Source: Eliot Marshall, *Science,* Vol. 236 (17 April 1987), pp. 250–251.

a shadow of a doubt the biological process by which sidestream smoke causes cancer. Nevertheless, studies have continued to accumulate information linking the likelihood of smoking-related diseases to the noxious chemicals found in sidestream smoke. Studies done in late 1989 and in 1990 have not only confirmed the conclusions the two 1986 reports reached, but have gone on to find further possible links.

One study of 674 women done in Utah in 1989, for example, found that women who were exposed to sidestream smoke on a regular basis were more likely to suffer cervical cancer than were those not exposed. [12] (The National Academy of Science report did not find a significant association between passive smoking and any cancers other than lung cancer.) Although clinical evidence suggests that cervical cancer results from a **virus**, researchers involved in the Utah study claim that passive smoking may make the cervix more vulnerable to viral infection. The study remains controversial and for the most part inconclusive. Skeptics claim that active and passive smokers may be more likely to have multiple sex partners than those who are not exposed to smoke, and that this is what increases one's likelihood of getting cervical cancer.

Although some studies remain inconclusive, the possibilities they present are frightening and have raised the ire of people who work or eat in the same restaurants as smokers. Lawmakers have

Virus: The smallest known type of infectious agent; viral infections range from minor conditions, such as the common cold, to fatal diseases, such as AIDS.

FIGURE 4.1
The Hazards of Sidestream Smoke

Children exposed to sidestream smoke on a regular basis have a lower rate of growth and are more likely to suffer from respiratory infection than children who are not.

concurred with this view. Within two years of the publication of the two reports, virtually every airline banned smoking on domestic airline flights shorter than two hours (this regulation has since been extended to cover all domestic flights). Many state-government-run and private companies posted stringent anti-smoking laws, limiting smoking only to designated areas, such as smoking lounges and private offices, and sometimes outlawing it altogether on company premises. Restaurants split their seating areas into nonsmoking and smoking sections and came under public pressure to eliminate smoking areas completely. Anti-smokers urging this say, and have hard evidence supporting them, that sharing air space with smokers—even if they are in separate areas—is a major health hazard.

But what of smokers' rights? Tobacco is, after all, a legal drug. They should, some smokers contend, have the right to

(continued on p. 75)

Did You Know That . . .

The rapidly accumulating evidence that secondhand smoke causes heart disease, stroke, and cancer in nonsmokers is causing many private companies to impose their own no-smoking rules.

The growing tendency to restrict smoking in the workplace has been criticized by some smokers. Among the arguments advanced by smokers is that they have a right to smoke. —[Ed.]

I am looking through the help-wanted ads in my local newspaper because I am thinking of going back to work. Limited by the narrow choice of offerings in the East End's primarily blue-collar work force, I scan each job description carefully.

An Office Casualty: My Right to Smoke

"Top-notch skills a must for busy real estate practice. Competitive salary. Nonsmoker."

"Part time for dynamic local petroleum distributor. Nonsmoking environment."

"Bright, efficient, reliable person for year-round office position. Heavy customer contact. Nonsmoking office."

Now my choice of jobs becomes even more paltry. No longer is it a question of matching my talents and abilities with an office that appreciates them; no longer is it a question of finding compatible surroundings. Now it's a question of where and where not I can smoke.

For the fact of the matter is, I smoke. Have smoked for 30 years. Smoked through college and graduate school, smoked through a successful career in advertising, smoked through a variety of challenging part-time jobs, smoked as a free-lance writer. Smoking was never a criterion of employment and, when I smoked, not to my recollection did anyone ever complain.

My professors and employers weren't interested in the quality of the air around me; they cared about the quality of my work. The bottom line was how well I did the job, not whether I smoked while doing it. As a productive and creative person, commanding me not to smoke would be as impertinent as ordering someone to go home and take a bath because she was wearing a heavy perfume.

Perhaps I am spoiled. As a writer, I've never considered writing "work." Writing is fun. It's an agreement with an editor to produce, by deadline, an informative story told in an interesting, responsible way. As a writer, I am asked, "Can you handle the assignment?" not, "Do you smoke?" Nor am I told that a nonsmoking writer is getting the assignment instead of me.

Through the years, I've become used to being treated as an adult, and I expect to be treated as the adult that I am. In modern maturity, I take responsibility for my own actions including, within reason, sleeping when I am tired, eating when I am hungry and smoking when I feel the need.

I pass by parking lots and see office employees sitting on benches or in cars, smoking, and hear about them tiptoeing off on "breaks" or sneaking a smoke in the bathrooms as if they were renegade high school punks. It is demeaning.

> No smoking in the workplace is the latest form of discrimination. Smokers are relegated to the parking lot instead of the back of the bus. Can you imagine an advertisement that instead of "nonsmoking office," dared say "nonfemale office" or "nonblack environment"?
>
> I don't like a room filled with tobacco smoke any more than the next person. But, with the proper ventilation, it need not be filled with smoke. Doubtless, there are negative effects from sitting next to an employee who smokes, but then there are also negative effects from sitting next to an employee who's sneezing from the cold or the flu.
>
> —*Alice Schultze*
>
> Source: Alice Schultze, *New York Times*, 27 March 1989, sec. 2, p. 13.

smoke it wherever and whenever they choose. Many people who smoke on the job depend on regular fixes of tobacco to help them concentrate. They want to smoke *while* they are working, at their own desks, and claim that it is their right. Some employees who work in open areas and are not allowed to smoke there are outraged that they must refrain from their habit while those with private offices—often executives within their own company—can smoke at their desks. [13] They see this as not only a smoking issue but a class issue as well. Some also believe it hints at racism. More executives are white than black or Hispanic, but the prevalence of smoking is higher among the latter two groups. [14] Many smokers think that the new law, in effect, discriminates against minorities who smoke and who are less likely to have their own offices.

Many people find it difficult to be without a cigarette on domestic airline flights. They resent the approval with which the antismoking contingent received the news of the airline regulations. People fly with colds and other contagious viral infections all the time, these people contend. Should they not be allowed to fly? In addition, say some, perfumes and colognes are as irritating to many as is cigarette smoke. If they are not limited, why should cigarettes be? Nevertheless, smokers have had to adhere to the new legislation designed to protect nonsmokers from the hazards of cigarettes.

TOBACCO AND PREGNANCY

Passive smokers are innocent victims of cigarette smoke and its potential health dangers. Without engaging in the habit them-

(continued on p. 77)

FIGURE 4.2
Why Start Life Under a Cloud?

Source: American Cancer Society.

Smoking during pregnancy can be harmful to the health and development of the unborn child. Among the health risks associated with smoking during pregnancy are premature birth, low birth weight, breathing difficulties, behavioral and learning problems, and hyperactivity.

selves, they are, often involuntarily, exposed to ETS. But passive smokers can do some things to protect themselves. They can often walk away from a smoker. They can request a friend to extinguish his or her cigarette. They can petition for more stringent antismoking laws. Unborn babies who come in contact with cigarette smoke can do none of these things. Instead, protecting an unborn child is left solely to the mother's discretion. If a pregnant woman chooses to smoke, she is placing her unborn child in grave danger of serious physical or mental damage.

Low Birth Weight

Cigarette smoking during pregnancy can cause **premature birth**, low birth weight, shorter body length, breathing difficulties at birth, behavioral and learning problems, and **hyperactivity**. The most frequent of these defects is low birth weight. This occurs when the fetus's growth and development within the mother's uterus is slowed or retarded, a condition known as **intrauterine growth retardation (IUGR)**. IUGR results when the flow of oxygen and nutrients to the fetus is cut off or interfered with. Hundreds of scientific surveys have studied the link between cigarette smoking and low birth weight. One of these reports surveyed 127,000 American women who became mothers between 1979 and 1985 and found that babies of women who smoked more than a pack of cigarettes a day during pregnancy were an average of 11.7 ounces lighter than the children of women who did not smoke. Five studies concerning 113,000 births in the United States, Canada, and Wales found that mothers who smoke lightly to moderately were 50 percent more likely—and those who smoke heavily twice as likely—to have babies weighing less than 5 pounds. [15]

Low birth weight can also cause a host of other problems. For example, it can increase the child's risk of suffering physical and mental defects, illnesses, learning disabilities, and behavioral problems. It can also lower the child's survival rate: the lower the child's weight at birth, the lower his or her chances of survival. The average weight of a newborn is between 7 and 9 pounds. Babies who weigh less than 5.8 pounds have a significant risk of dying. Those weighing 3.5 pounds or less are in very grave danger indeed.

Premature Birth

Smoking increases the likelihood of vaginal bleeding during pregnancy, which can in turn lead to premature birth. Even if bleeding does not occur, studies show that premature birth occurs

Premature birth: A birth that occurs before completion of the normal nine-month gestation period.

Hyperactivity: A behavioral pattern in children characterized by overactivity and inability to concentrate.

Intrauterine growth retardation (IUGR): An abnormally low rate of fetal growth and development caused either by undernourishment or a physical defect in the fetus.

Infertility and Smoking

We know that a pregnant woman's smoking can harm her unborn baby, and that the smoke inhaled from parental cigarettes can impair an infant's health. Can the habit also hurt a couple's chance of conceiving a child in the first place?

While it has not been proved that smoking leads to infertility, a relationship has long been suspected, and several studies have strongly suggested a cause-and-effect relationship.

In one recently reported study, a team from the National Institute of Environmental Health Sciences investigated the time required for 678 women to become pregnant after they had stopped using birth control because they wanted to conceive.

The results: during the first menstrual cycle, 38 percent of the nonsmokers conceived, but only 28 percent of the smokers did so. And the smokers were 3.4 times more likely to take more than a year to become pregnant. The researchers estimated that smokers were only 72 percent as fertile as nonsmokers and that those who smoked more than a pack a day had only 57 percent of the fertility of nonsmokers.

Their conclusion: "Reduced fertility should be added to the growing list of reproductive hazards of cigarette smoking."

Does the hazard persist? Or does an ex-smoker regain a non-smoker's chances of conceiving? Among the women studied, 31 had stopped smoking within the year before attempting to become pregnant. These women did not experience reduced fertility. The investigators cautioned, however, that the number was too small to interpret definitively.

Source: Dodi Schultz, *Priorities* (Winter 1989), p. 5.

---

10 percent more frequently among moderate smokers and 20 percent more frequently among heavy smokers than among nonsmokers. [16] Premature babies not only are underweight but can suffer a host of problems, such as underdevelopment of the respiratory tract, nervous system, muscles, and other organs. Cigarettes also increase a woman's risk of suffering a **miscarriage** or stillbirth or of the child dying during his or her first weeks of life. According to studies, smokers have a 30 to 70 percent greater chance of suffering a miscarriage than nonsmokers, depending in part on the number of cigarettes smoked each day. One study found that smoking a pack a day or more virtually doubled the risk of miscarriage. [17] Smoking also

Miscarriage: Loss of the fetus before it can survive outside the mother's uterus.

FIGURE 4.3
Low Birth Weight and Smoking

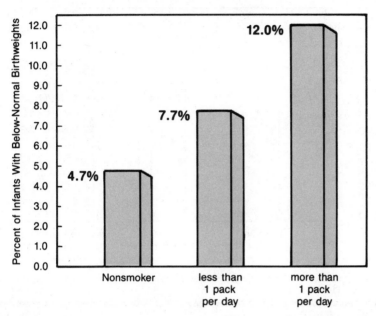

Source: *The Health Consequences of Smoking for Women,* Department of Health and Human Services, 1981.

Infants whose mothers smoke more than one pack of cigarettes per day are more than twice as likely to be underweight at birth as infants born to nonsmoking mothers.

increases the rate of stillbirths, particularly among women who are receiving poor prenatal care because of socioeconomic factors, such as poverty or lack of education. [18]

Respiratory Infections and Other Illnesses
Children of smokers are especially susceptible to certain health ailments. Earlier we saw that passive smoking increases a child's susceptibility to respiratory infection. The same holds true for the children of mothers who smoked during pregnancy even if they have quit since giving birth. Several studies have shown that these babies have more illnesses before the age of 5 than do the children of nonsmokers. They have a significantly higher fre-

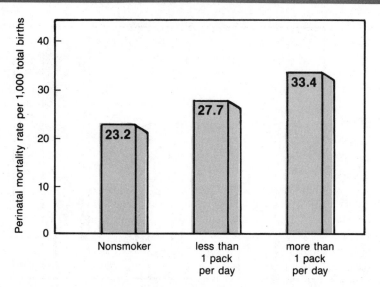

FIGURE 4.4
Perinatal Mortality and Smoking

Source: *The Health Consequences of Smoking for Women,* Department of Health and Human Services, 1981.

Women who smoke one or more packs of cigarettes a day have approximately a 50 percent greater chance of losing their child during or prior to birth.

quency of colds, for example, which can in turn lead to more serious problems, such as lung and ear infections. [19] Researchers have also found that the babies of smokers suffer a higher rate of bronchitis and pneumonia during their first year of life.

The risk of illness is not limited to the respiratory system. There is evidence that the babies of mothers who smoked during pregnancy are as much as 50 percent more likely to suffer childhood cancers such as **leukemia** than the children of nonsmoking mothers. Many studies have found that these babies have an increased likelihood of suffering behavioral problems, such as hyperactivity. This disorder is characterized by excitability, concentration problems, and overactivity.

Congenital Deformities

It has not been definitively proven that cigarette smoking during

Leukemia: Any of several types of cancer caused by an overproduction of destructive white blood cells, which impairs the production of red blood cells and platelets, and normal white blood cells.

pregnancy can cause **congenital deformities**, but some studies have found that children of mothers who smoke may have a higher frequency of heart malformations, abnormally small jaws and mouths, and upturned noses than those of nonsmokers. Several studies have found that smoking mothers who also take tranquilizers have a decidedly higher risk of bearing a deformed child than do mothers who do not take any drugs. Scientists are continuing to conduct surveys of smoking mothers to determine more conclusively if there is a link between smoking and congenital malformations.

Chemicals That Cross the Placenta

Scientists have studied not only the ways cigarette smoking can damage an unborn child, but the reasons these problems occur. In chapter 3 we discussed the chemical makeup of cigarette smoke, which is comprised of nearly 4,000 different compounds, such as nicotine and carbon monoxide. It also contains some heavy metals, such as cadmium and lead.

These two elements enter the blood every time a cigarette smoker inhales, and they can cause grave damage to the **placenta**. In animal studies, even low doses of cadmium resulted in low birth weights. In these same animal studies, at high concentrations cadmium caused miscarriages, stillbirths, and malformed offspring. Lead can interfere with the fetus's enzyme systems; studies show that babies born to smoking mothers have a significantly reduced enzyme activity compared to those of nonsmokers.

Cyanide from cigarette smoke also travels to the bloodstream. The body's metabolic process quickly converts this chemical to **thiocyanate**, a substance that is normally present in the human body in minute quantities from the foods we eat. But cyanide and thiocyanate are both toxic compounds and at higher levels can reduce the ability of cells to use oxygen, interfere with the body's ability to process vitamin B_{12}, and damage brain cells. Many scientists believe that thiocyanate is a significant cause of low birth weight babies among smokers.

Nicotine and carbon monoxide are the two most studied chemicals in cigarette smoke. Both cross the placenta. Nicotine causes blood vessels to narrow, including those that carry blood through the placenta. As a result, blood flow to the placenta is reduced, lessening the organ's ability to supply nutrients to the unborn child. You may recall from chapter 3 that carboxyhemoglobin forms when carbon monoxide bonds to hemoglobin. The blood of a smoker contains 4 to 5 times the amount of this

Congenital deformities: Birth defects; physical or mental abnormalities arising before birth from either a genetic defect or intrauterine damage.

Placenta: The intrauterine organ that joins the maternal and fetal blood supplies during pregnancy.

Cyanide: A group of often highly toxic chemical compounds containing cyanogen.

Thiocyanate: A substance, found in many foods, that can be toxic if administered in large doses.

FIGURE 4.5
Smoking and the Fetus

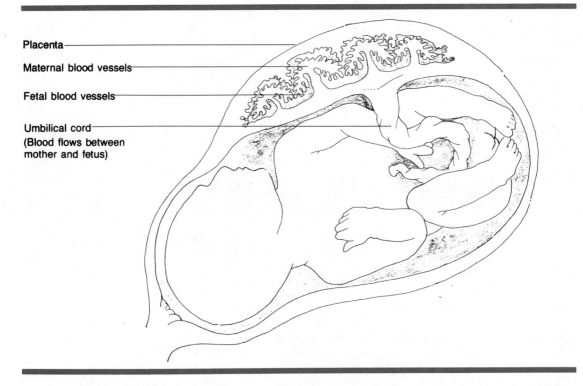

Placenta

Maternal blood vessels

Fetal blood vessels

Umbilical cord
(Blood flows between
mother and fetus)

The fetus receives nourishment from the mother by means of the umbilical cord which is attached to the placenta. Unfortunately, toxic substances found in cigarette smoke such as nicotine, cyanide, carbon monoxide, and lead can and do reach the developing fetus by the same route.

compound as does that of a nonsmoker, and the level of carbox-yhemoglobin in the fetus runs 10 percent to 20 percent higher than in its mother. The presence of carboxyhemoglobin interferes with the flow of oxygen and nutrients to the fetus, which we know is a major cause of IUGR and low birth weight.

It is easy to conclude from the studies done on passive smokers and the children of smoking mothers that nobody should smoke cigarettes, period. Indeed, that is a goal C. Everett Koop has set for the twenty-first century (see chapter 1). Chapter 5 discusses the ways in which health advocates are attempting to prevent people from starting to smoke and examines whether these efforts have been successful. 𝕎

Prevention

WHY DO PEOPLE START TO SMOKE, and what can society do to prevent this? In general, prevention efforts come in two forms and target two separate groups. The first of these are education programs, which are designed to teach students from kindergarten through high school the dangers and unattractive aspects of smoking. These programs are important because, according to studies, 80 percent of those who are habitual smokers start smoking before the age of 21. [1]

This is unsurprising to a certain extent. **Adolescence** is a time of intense change. Often teenagers feel stranded between childhood and adulthood and choose behaviors that seem more grown-up to them. Smoking, with its aura of maturity and sophistication, is an obvious temptation. In addition, young people apply an immense amount of **peer pressure** to each other. Teenagers who would otherwise have no desire to smoke may start a cigarette habit in order to feel more accepted and then may start pressuring their friends to do the same.

The second form of prevention targets everyone, but may be especially important to those who are uneducated and in lower socioeconomic brackets. The 1989 Surgeon General's report states that not only do the uneducated have the lowest decline in smoking, but that there are no specific prevention programs designed to help them. **Health advocates** are attempting to make up for this inequity by sponsoring legislation to limit cigarette advertising and to make cigarettes, which have always been relatively inexpensive and easily accessible, much harder to get.

Adolescence: The period of intense change that marks the transition between childhood and adulthood.

Peer pressure: Pressure placed on a person by his or her contemporaries to participate in a given activity, such as smoking, drinking alcohol, or taking other psychoactive substances.

Health advocates: Professionals, usually in the health field, involved in actions dedicated to improving the general health of the nation.

(continued on p. 86)

Why Are Girls Smoking More Than Guys?

As a teenager, I decided I wanted to smoke after watching *Now Voyager*, an old Bette Davis movie in which she and Paul Henreid play star-crossed lovers. You get the first tingle of their mutual attraction in the scene where Henreid puts two cigarettes in his mouth, lights them both, and gives her one. Then they smoke and look smolderingly at each other for a while. I could've *died* from the heat coming off the screen. It was so romantic. Glamorous. Sophisticated. *Sexy.* The only way I could hope to be that cool would be to learn to smoke as well.

Fortunately for my health, I could never quite get the hang of smoking. May I confess that I couldn't inhale without feeling a deep desire to blow my lunch? On the spot? Which was definitely *not* romantic, glamorous, sophisticated, or sexy. My smoking days were nipped in the bud, but apparently there are a lot of you out there who don't suffer from my weak stomach. The American Cancer Society reports that although smoking has declined among teenagers on the whole, teenage girls are now the fastest-growing group of smokers, and they now smoke *more* than teenage boys do.

Among high school seniors, 28 percent of both boys and girls smoked daily in 1976. By 1984 smoking among boys had declined to 16%, but among girls it was down much less—only 20.5 percent.

Now we all know about the health hazards of smoking, we've all read the surgeon general's warning—so why are girls still smoking more? One major reason is that times have changed.

It used to be that smoking was considered "unladylike" and that only "bad" or "fast" girls smoked. (The flappers of the twenties smoked because it was such a shocking thing to do then.) But with the feminist movement in the sixties and seventies, smoking became commonplace among women. "Female cigarette smoking reflects an expression of the liberation ethic," says Lloyd Johnston, PH.D., of the Institute for Social Research at the University of Michigan, in Ann Arbor. "Women see it as a way of expressing independence and worldliness."

Now, the tobacco industry is not stupid. It saw this trend and realized it had a huge new untapped market for its product. Since the early seventies the industry has been tailoring its advertisements to appeal to young women. There's the Virginia Slims "You've come a long way, baby" campaign, which tells girls that contemporary, independent women smoke. The Salem ads, in which attractive, healthy couples frolic on the beach, say subliminally that smoking is wholesome and will get you a cute boyfriend. These ads are geared to appeal more to girls than to boys.

The ads are also targeted for young people because, according to Karen Monaco of the American Lung Association, 90 percent of all smokers make their decision to start by the age of nineteen. Forty-nine percent of the high school seniors who are pack-a-day smokers started by the ninth grade. "The tobacco industry is obviously going for the youth market—and not just through ads," says Monaco. "Cigarette companies also do a lot of special promotions—such as sponsoring rock concerts, car racing, sporting events—that appeal to young people."

So the tobacco industry is going for women, and it is going for young people. Bingo: Teenage girls are now the hottest market, and unfortunately the prosmoking message seems to be getting through. Many girls still see smoking as one way to look cool and appear older, and they will make enormous efforts to learn how to puff.

Laurie Shaw, seventeen, from the Bronx, New York, started smoking at thirteen because she wanted to fit in with an older crowd. "I had trouble inhaling," she recalls, "so I had a friend hold my nose, and then I'd breathe in. It made me sick."

Karen Warner, sixteen, from Portland, Oregon, didn't want to smoke in front of her friends until she could do it right. "You could tell if kids were smoking and they couldn't inhale," she says. "We all thought they were jerks, so I wanted to make sure I learned how." She accomplished that by stealing her mother's cigarette butts out of the ashtrays and then practicing while leaning out of her bedroom window.

This behavior is glamorous? Attractive? If the above hasn't convinced you otherwise, allow me to debunk *that* myth once and for all. The American Lung Association has conducted a study that is going to surprise you. In a 1986 national survey 78 percent of teenage boys polled said they preferred to date a nonsmoker. Only 1 percent said they preferred to date a smoker. (The rest said it made no difference to them.) You may have come a long way, baby, but has anyone warm and snugly come along with you?

This brings me to another myth I'd like to explode. Some girls think there is one positive physical effect of smoking. It's probably a main reason they start or don't quit smoking: They believe it will keep them thin, and they're afraid they'll gain weight if they stop. True, smokers on the whole are slightly thinner than nonsmokers. But the fact is, the weight difference is only a few pounds, and as Monaco says, "There are so many better ways to control your weight that don't involve a lifelong addiction to an unhealthy substance."

Monaco also reports that some scientists believe weight gain after quitting is due to the fact that nicotine affects the level of blood sugar in the body and that nicotine withdrawal triggers an increased craving for sweet foods. It's not just that you eat more when you quit but that you eat more sugar. If you are conscious of this and substitute other foods for the sweets, weight gain should be negligible.

There's another reason teenagers smoke. Despite all the media attention focused on the hazards of smoking, most kids don't think anything bad will ever happen to them.

"When you're young, you never think that you're going to die or that you'll develop a disease," notes Dr. Richard Feldman, director of family practice residency at St. Francis Hospital in Beech Grove, Indiana. "Most teenagers think they won't get hooked, so they don't have to worry about long-term effects. The fact is, they're playing with fire, because they do get hooked. I've seen it happen over and over again."

Kelly Morris of New York, who started smoking when she was eight, had been warned about the side effects of smoking, to no avail. "People always said it would stunt my growth, but I'd say, 'Well, I didn't want to be tall, anyway,' " she says with a laugh. She has been smoking steadily for ten years now and has found it very difficult to quit.

Samantha Christopher from Shawnee, Oklahoma, was even more reckless. "I have a history of cancer in my family," she says, "but I thought those people must have smoked a lot more than *I* intended to. I just figured I was too young to worry about it." At nineteen, Samantha has just quit smoking after a two-year habit. "I realized how bad it was for me and for the people around me."

The health risks of smoking *should* concern you, even if you are young. If you get hooked, the long-range effects can be lung cancer or emphysema, among a myriad of other diseases. In fact, last year for the first time more women in the United States died of lung cancer than breast cancer.

But even if you don't become addicted, there are short-term effects to worry about.

Fact: If you are athletic, you'll find your stamina is drastically reduced. Hannah Franklin, seventeen, from Westwood, Massachusetts, was a track star until she started smoking. "I was getting so winded," she says. "I really had to cut way back on my smoking in order to get back up to my previous performance level. I finally quit smoking altogether."

Fact: Studies indicate that there are cardiovascular risks for teenage girls who smoke and take birth control pills. This connection gets stronger as you get older.

Fact: Bad breath, numb taste buds, yellow teeth, and stained fingers are unhealthy and *totally* unappealing.

Do you still think smoking is the key to looking sophisticated? It might have worked for Bette Davis way back when, but snoods and penciled eyebrows were considered pretty racy then too. If *Now Voyager* were being made today, Paul Henreid would probably lace up Davis's aerobics sneakers before he'd ever light her cigarette.

Source: Beth Levine, *Seventeen* (January 1988), pp. 78–79, 97.

Table 5.1 Use of Cigarettes in a Given Month by Youths 12–17 Years of Age and Young Adults 18–25 Years of Age, According to Age and Sex: United States, Selected Years 1972–85

[Data are based on household interviews of a sample of the population 12 years of age and over in the coterminous United States]

Substance, Age, and Sex	1972	1974	1976	1977	1979	1982	1985
Cigarettes				**Percent of Population**			
Both sexes:							
12–17 years	(1)	25	23	22	(1)	15	15
12–13 years	(1)	13	11	10	(1)	*3	6
14–15 years	(1)	25	20	22	(1)	10	14
16–17 years	(1)	38	39	35	(1)	30	25
18–25 years	(1)	49	49	47	(1)	40	37
Male:							
12–17 years	(1)	27	21	23	(1)	16	16
18–25 years	(1)	50	48	50	(1)	37	38
Female:							
12–17 years	(1)	24	26	22	(1)	13	15
18–25 years	(1)	47	51	44	(1)	42	35

[1]Data not comparable because definitions differ.

*Relative standard error greater than 30 percent.

Source: *Health United States,* No. 0052, 1988, p. 97.

This table, depicting the smoking habits of a selected group of men and women during a specific month of a chosen year, shows how significantly the percentage of smokers declined between 1972 and 1985.

EDUCATIONAL PROGRAMS

According to the American Cancer Society (ACS), each day more than 3,000 adolescents smoke their first cigarette. This adds up to more than a million new smokers each year. [2] For this reason, when the American Cancer Society established priorities for its public education programs, it placed efforts to prevent smoking at the top of its list. [3] The ACS, the American Heart Association, and several other associations have developed antismoking educational programs aimed at preventing young students from starting to smoke and helping those who are already smoking to quit.

The ACS programs reflect the association's resolve that children are never too young to be aware of health hazards; their "Starting Free" program is designed especially for preschoolers.

The "Starting Free" package includes five pamphlets for teachers and parents to read to children. The pamphlets aim to heighten the child's awareness of his or her smoking world, including the differences between "good air" and "bad air." The accompanying facilitator's guide stresses that it is never too early to start emphasizing smoking prevention; an astonishing 41 percent of American children have tried a cigarette by the time they are of preschool age. [4] "Our feeling is that these kids should know about cigarettes and their dangers while they're young," says ACS health educator Karen Rosenfeld. "By the time they are teenagers, it might be too late."

The ACS does have prevention and **cessation** programs for older children, however. One of these, "Breaking Free," is a combined prevention-cessation package aimed at high school vocational students. "Breaking Free" includes a comic-book rendition and a video cassette featuring two teenagers who resolve to quit smoking together and enjoy a much healthier, happier life once they have kicked their habit. In its teacher's guide, "Breaking Free" lists several hard facts about smoking. These are not only basic information about the health hazards attached to tobacco, but also specific statistics that concern vocational students, a much higher percentage of whom smoke than students in college-preparatory programs. The back of the guide also lists suggestions on how to break a smoking habit.

Another program is the "Smoke-free Class of 2000," which is a cooperative effort of the American Cancer Society, the American Heart Association, and the American Lung Association. This prevention program follows the children in the class (those born in 1983) from kindergarten to third grade and provides a specific curriculum for them to study during each of these years. During the course of the program the children are asked to perform plays, draw antismoking posters and signs, and write compositions on the dangers of cigarette smoking. Then, at the end of each year, there is a celebration and ceremony marking the children's graduation from each grade. "The plan is to keep momentum going for these kids during preschool and early schooling," says ACS's Rosenfeld. "The course resumes at the beginning of each year, so that by the end of the program the children are completely aware of the dangers of cigarettes, and are, we believe, dead set against it." Rosenfeld also stresses that it is too early to know how effective the "Smoke-free Class of 2000" will be. Those sponsoring the program are inspired by the response it has received so far. In 1989, 100,000 students from 4,000 schools participated in the program in New York City alone. Because of

(continued on p. 89)

Did You Know That . . .

Although it is illegal to sell cigarettes to minors in most states, an estimated 927 million packs are sold to young people aged 18 and below each year.

Cessation: A stop; the temporary or permanent ceasing of a habit such as smoking.

FIGURE 5.1
Smoking Cessation Programs

The American Cancer Society, the American Lung Association, and the American Heart Association offer a variety of programs to help smokers quit and to encourage young people not to start smoking.

these numbers, "Smokefree Class of 2000" has become a full part of the curriculum in a high percentage of these schools, which will be offering it to grades kindergarten through third for many years to come.

Since 1983, the American Heart Association has sponsored "Save a Sweet Heart," a multileveled program designed for preschool, lower and upper elementary school, middle school, and high school students. A four-week event usually scheduled around Valentine's Day, "Save a Sweet Heart" is designed to create a positive nonsmoking atmosphere and to provide a supportive environment for smokers who want to quit. The program lists three main objectives: 1) to build an awareness of the dangers of smoking; 2) to provide nonsmoking images and school support for the decision to be smoke-free; and 3) to create an opportunity for all students to pledge formally either not to start smoking during the next year or not to smoke on SASH day, a predesignated day chosen at the program's beginning.

The main feature of the "Save a Sweet Heart" program is a comprehensive teacher's guide that includes specific information linking smoking to heart disease and activities the class can participate in. For example, the high school version of the program suggests dividing the class into groups that would research and then represent the viewpoints of both tobacco-related groups, such as growers, distributors, and retailers, and advocates trying to pass legislation regulating smoking in public places.

By the end of the four-week period, students should be able to list three harmful substances in cigarette smoke, list at least seven physical hazards of smoking, recognize the advantages of being a nonsmoker, identify reasons why teenagers start smoking, and recognize that the decision to smoke is influenced by outside forces, such as peer pressure and advertising.

THE EDUCATIONAL AND RACIAL FACTORS

Educational prevention programs have been moderately successful deterrents for those who stay in school. Unfortunately, those who are most likely to smoke, according to studies, are those who do not graduate from high school. [5] For example, in 1985, 18.4 percent of college graduates smoked, whereas 34.2 percent of those who had not completed high school smoked. [6] The heartening news is that both percentages have decreased since 1974, when the numbers were, respectively, 28.5 percent and 36.3 percent. It is evident from the significantly higher decrease

(continued on p. 91)

FIGURE 5.2
Lung Cancer Death Rates

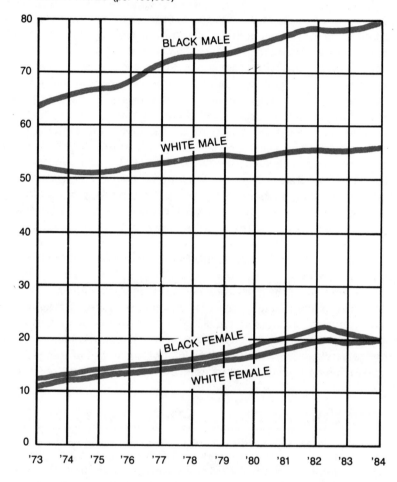

DEATH RATES (per 100,000)

Source: National Center for Health Statistics.

Lung cancer death rates among blacks are significantly higher than among whites and the difference appears to be increasing. In recent years, the lung cancer death rate among black men has increased three times faster than among white males. It is currently unclear, however, whether this difference is caused by racial or socio-economic factors.

among the more educated group, however, that a serious disparity remains.

This situation has some serious consequences. Blacks and other minorities tend to be less educated and in a lower socioeconomic bracket than white people. Unsurprisingly, therefore, these first two groups have a higher percentage of smokers and may be more susceptible targets of cigarette advertising. Tobacco companies have been accused of taking advantage of this situation and targeting minority groups in many of their cigarette campaigns. The most extreme case of this occurred in 1989, when one tobacco company devised and marketed a brand of cigarettes specifically for blacks. Public uproar followed and the company quickly withdrew the product. On a more subtle note, an increasing number of cigarette advertisements feature blacks and Hispanics "enjoying" a smoke. Billboards featuring tobacco advertisements are becoming more and more prevalent in inner-city neighborhoods. As a result, young children are involuntarily exposed to promotions expounding the virtues of smoking.

Expressing his concern, American Cancer Society national president Harold Freeman stated that "the cigarette industry just wants to make money because they know that poor and uneducated people are their main customers. And black people are disproportionately poor and uneducated." [7] Philip Morris Company representative Steve Weiss denied this charge, noting that his company "advertises cigarettes to those who smoke, regardless of race and background." [8] As a preventive measure, legislators have moved to pass some laws requiring tobacco companies to cut down on this form of promotion. One such proposal, suggested by Baltimore lobbyists, would be a law providing economic incentive for cities to replace tobacco advertisements with ones concerning public safety. There are no such laws as of yet.

TOBACCO AND ADVERTISING

The issue of billboards is only a small part of the controversy concerning cigarettes and advertising. Those concerned with prevention believe that far fewer people would smoke if cigarette advertisements were banned completely. They point to the significant decline in cigarette consumption after 1969, when national legislation banned all cigarette commercials from radio and television. This sentiment gathered momentum in 1987, after the publication of the 1986 reports on the dangers of passive smok-

Did You Know That . . .

The tobacco industry is the single largest purchaser of magazine and billboard advertising space in the United States.

First Amendment: The section of the Bill of Rights stating that all Americans have the right to practice freedom of speech, freedom of the press, and freedom of religion.

American Bar Association (ABA): An organization comprised of practicing American lawyers.

ing. Led by then-Surgeon General C. Everett Koop, antismoking activists began lobbying Congress to pass legislation outlawing all forms of advertising for tobacco, including window displays in stores that sell it.

This action met with some passionate opposition. Obviously, the tobacco companies were displeased, stressing that there is little or no proof that advertising increases the sale of their product. Any legal action to limit, censor, or outlaw such advertising, they added, would be an infringement of freedom of speech, guaranteed by the Constitution's **First Amendment**. Tobacco companies were not alone. The Health-Protection Act, the bill proposed to outlaw tobacco advertisements, failed to win the approval of the **American Bar Association (ABA)**. The ABA not only disapproved of the bill for reasons concerning the first amendment, but it expressed fear that such potential censorship could spread to other issues. [9] Congress then refused to pass the bill on the grounds that it would not be lawful to prohibit advertising for a product that was itself not unlawful. In other words, because cigarettes are legal, advertisements that promote them should remain legal as well.

Two years later the issue came up again. In one of his final publications as surgeon general, C. Everett Koop urged Congress to consider again a ban on tobacco advertising. The paper, published in the *Journal of the American Medical Association* (JAMA), stressed that although there are as of yet no studies proving conclusively that advertising tobacco products increases their sales, the burden to prove a possible link should not be on the health advocates. Rather, it should be up to tobacco companies and their advertisers to prove that such an association does *not* exist. [10] Koop also responded to both the case for freedom of speech and the right to advertise a legal product. We do not, he states, have the right to publish lies or deceptive advertisements. A billboard showing a package of cigarettes, a young couple, and the slogan "Alive With Pleasure" is more than just a plug for a product. It is, Koop argues, a downright lie. [11]

Congress has yet to pass new legislation limiting tobacco advertising, but other countries have taken the initiative and no longer permit cigarette promotions. Nigeria, where 1.7 million people depend on tobacco farming and sales for their livelihood, [12] prohibited tobacco commercials, billboard messages, and newspaper advertisements in 1988. One reason for this action, according to Nigerian spokespeople, was that international tobacco companies had targeted their country as a new market for their product. Also in 1988, India, where 800,000 people die each

(continued on p. 94)

Life without tobacco . . . isn't just something the typical two-pack-a-day smoker is pondering.

It's a multi-million dollar question magazine publishers across the U.S. are trying to answer as pressures to ban cigarette ads increase in Congress.

Life (the magazine, that is) would stand to lose annual advertising

Life Without Tobacco Advertising

revenues of $6.2 million if the magazine could no longer accept cigarette ads. That would mean a loss of one-eighth of the publication's total ad revenue, not a fatal blow, but a serious wound.

More serious would be the impact of a loss of tobacco advertising to magazines such as *Penthouse*, where advertising revenue from tobacco represents 25.3 percent of its income from all advertising.

Among the hardest hit by a loss of tobacco ad revenue would be the nation's three major news magazines: *Time, Newsweek* and *U.S. News,* which currently receive a combined total of $48.1 million per year in tobacco advertising revenue.

Proposed bans on tobacco advertising have surfaced in the past, but [a] growing number of bills which would restrict or ban the promotion and advertising of tobacco products are pending in Congress.

Among the most feared by the advertising industry is a proposal by Senator Ted Kennedy (D-Mass) which would repeal the federal pre-emption of state restrictions on tobacco advertising. If this bill passes, it could result in a de facto ban on national tobacco ads.

This time it isn't just the anti-smoking groups pushing for tobacco ad restrictions. Health and Human Services Secretary Louis Sullivan has become an outspoken ally since it was revealed that R. J. Reynolds had targeted "Uptown" at urban blacks.

In addition, Federal Trade Commission Chairman Janet Steiger shocked the advertising industry in a recent speech when she advised agencies that they would be held liable for deceptive or unfair advertising practices.

Mrs. Steiger, after a cautious initial first five months at the FTC, named several marketing targets high on her agenda. In keeping with earlier remarks, many of those are in the tobacco and alcohol categories.

"I am concerned that some members of the tobacco industry appear to believe they can target 18-year-old smokers without a substantial risk that the same advertising will prove highly attractive to younger teenagers, or even preteens," she said.

"And the possible effects of these practices in the tobacco industry may be magnified by other marketing practices that may result in cigarettes being too readily available to underage consumers."

Did You Know That . . .

Television and radio cigarette advertising was banned in 1971. Similar action against ads for smokeless tobacco was taken in 1986.

In that regard, she cited such examples as "free samples distributed outside rock concerts or other youth events, certain couponing activities and reported non-compliance by many retailers with state laws restricting the sale of cigarettes to minors."

Mrs. Steiger also expressed concern over college promotions for alcoholic beverages. "I have asked my staff to scrutinize carefully advertising and promotional activities for these (alcohol and tobacco) products and to develop promptly law enforcement recommendations about any activity that violates the FTC's proscription against unfair or deceptive practices."

According to leading advertising and publishing analysts, there is no longer a question whether tobacco advertising will be banned. It's only a matter of when the ban will be implemented.

And, the liquor industry is watching current developments on tobacco advertising restrictions with more than a passing interest. If the advertising industry can learn to survive without tobacco revenue, could they manage without alcohol revenue as well?

Source: *Monday Morning Report,* Vol. 13, No. 13, 26 March 1990 (Alcohol Research Information Service, Lansing, Michigan).

year of tobacco-related diseases, [13] banned tobacco advertising in the hope that it would prevent their youth from starting to smoke.

American health advocates will no doubt be watching the results of advertising bans in these two countries; if such a policy proves successful, pressure on Congress to pass similar legislation will certainly increase dramatically.

ANTISMOKING ACTIONS

In the meantime, state and local governments are passing some laws to limit the access to cigarettes. In 1989, New York City banned the use of cigarette vending machines. A year earlier, the city had restricted smoking in most public places. In 1988 the University of Kentucky made a daring move when it approved restrictions of smoking on campus. This action met with serious opposition from state lawmakers, who stated that such a policy threatened students' individual rights. They were also admittedly concerned about the ways such a policy would affect the state economically. The tobacco industry accounts for 54,000 jobs in Kentucky, and tobacco is the state's number one cash crop. [14] But university officials have not rescinded their restrictions.

(continued on p. 97)

Clearing the Air in the Schools

The signs ringing New Jersey's schools that indicate that one is entering a "drug-free school zone" proclaim a worthy goal. A bill recently passed the Assembly by a 59–10 vote that would move our schools significantly closer to becoming genuinely drug-free. Of equal importance, the bill controls tobacco smoke pollution in the public schools and abates the health hazard this material causes.

The bill, by Assemblywoman Maureen Ogden and Assemblyman Harold L. Colburn, Jr., requires local boards of education to make schools completely smoke-free. This removes what has been a frustrating stumbling block, namely, the contention that this is an issue that must be settled by labor negotiations. The state's teachers' unions have opposed the efforts of several local boards to become smoke-free because they have maintained that this is a negotiable item, a position that ignores the overriding health and educational aspects of the problem.

Nearly all New Jersey schools permit smoking by faculty and staff members somewhere in the buildings, and a recent survey conducted by the Commission on Smoking or Health found that 40 percent of high schools also set aside areas for students to smoke.

The current law regulating smoking in schools is [ten] years old. It was written and passed well before the 1986 Surgeon General's report on involuntary smoking, which concluded that tobacco smoke pollution is a cause of lung cancer in nonsmokers.

Furthermore, the report indicated that the only way to prevent the risk posed by this carcinogen is for buildings to be smoke-free. Buildings generally have but one common air space, which is shared by all rooms, and filtration and dilution do not provide sufficient cleansing to remove the carcinogens present in smoke.

Since the 1986 report was prepared, additional studies of tobacco smoke pollution have been done, and it is now clear that this material also increases the risk of cancers other than lung cancer and also increases the risk of fatal heart attacks in nonsmokers. In fact, the scientific evidence of harm to nonsmokers from tobacco smoke is far stronger than is the evidence that either asbestos or radon poses dangers to the general public at environmental levels of exposure. The efforts to control asbestos and radon exposure are appropriate. What this means, though, is that we should pay much more attention to abating tobacco smoke in the environment than we have up to now.

Permitting smoking in schools also undermines a school's educational objectives about tobacco and other drugs. Today's educational message about tobacco is that no one should ever use this material. It is highly addictive, and it is harmful to those around a person who smokes. The fact that its use is not only tolerated but actually accommodated in schools by faculty and staff members and students contradicts this message and also is frequently seen by students as an example of adult hypocrisy about other drug abuse.

The educational message about alcohol sharply contrasts with what the schools are teaching about tobacco. Alcohol can be safely used by most people when they are of age and when specific guidelines for use are followed. In contrast, it is impossible to use tobacco safely. Based on these educational messages alone (apart from the other issues raised), it makes more sense to have faculty cocktail lounges in our schools than it does to have smoking lounges.

Half of adult cigarette smoking begins by age 13, 70 percent by age 15 and 90 percent by age 19. Nicotine addiction is a disease of childhood and adolescence, and our schools must become more effective in preventing this drug dependence. For many years, physicians and nurses . . . have been expected not to smoke in front of patients because of the double message involved. Teachers and school staffs, too, should be expected to follow this straightforward principle.

It is illegal to sell or give tobacco products to anyone under age 18 in [New Jersey]. Sanctioned smoking areas for students in our schools obviously mock the law. At the same time, the double standard of having no smoking for students and permitting smoking for faculty fosters justifiable resentment among students.

Other institutions are moving rapidly toward becoming smoke-free. The New Jersey Hospital Association, in cooperation with the State Department of Health, recently initiated a consultation service to help the state's hospitals accomplish this. Seven have already become smoke-free, and 41 others will be doing this in coming months. The Department of Health is smoke-free, as are the Medical Society of New Jersey and the offices of the New Jersey School Boards Association.

In Minnesota, more than two-thirds of all school districts have become tobacco-free in only two years as the result of a statewide consultation service encouraging this. Hundreds of businesses in New Jersey and elsewhere have taken this step because of the health and morale issues it addresses.

Smoke-free policies are popular and effective if they are thoughtfully developed and implemented. They are well accepted among people who smoke, probably for two reasons. First, most who smoke understand and sympathize with the problems and hazards that tobacco smoke creates for nonsmokers, and, second, the overwhelming majority of people who smoke want to quit. Many come to see smoke-free policies as a way to gain some control over their addiction to nicotine.

Many national organizations, including the National Education Association, support the creation of smoke-free schools. The New Jersey School Boards Association and the New Jersey P.T.A. support smoke-free schools, although the School Boards Association prefers a voluntary approach.

The voluntary health agencies in New Jersey that deal with the diseases tobacco causes, the Cancer Society, the Lung Association and the Heart Association, support efforts to create smoke-free schools; this policy complements the significant tobacco use prevention work these organizations are doing in the state's schools. The New Jersey Group Against Smoke Pollution has compiled a directory of schools in the state that have already become smoke-free, and it is actively working with several local boards to help them become smoke-free despite the opposition of their teachers' bargaining units.

The Assembly bill is an important measure, and the commission strongly urges that it become law. The health and educational issues involved are important enough that smoke-free schools should be required by law. Senator Donald T. DiFrancesco has introduced a parallel measure in the upper house. We urge timely passage by that body.

Even these bills omit one key element for success, however. Achieving smoke-free schools is certainly possible, and a lot is already known about how to best create and implement a successful policy. In Minnesota, the widespread, rapid achievement of smoke-free schools has been fostered by a consultant in the State Department of Education who has provided technical support and inspiration to local boards working on this problem. Such a service should obviously be created within our own Department of Education as well, especially since all boards in the state would be making this transition under the proposal.

As with the hospitals, many school districts are interested in becoming smoke-free, but they are holding back. Passage of the bills and the creation of a consultation service in the Department of Education are essential for overcoming this hesitation. The bills will remove this issue from the arena of labor negotiations and place the matter in the realms of educational policy and occupational safety and health, where it belongs.

This, in turn, will bring our schools closer to becoming drug-free, and those blue-on-white reflectorized signs will become much more truthful.

—John Slade

Source: John Slade, *New York Times*, 23 April 1989 (New Jersey Supplement), sec. 12, p. 24.

FIGURE 5.3
Dr. C. Everett Koop

Source: Office of Dr. C. Everett Koop.

As Surgeon General of the United States from 1981 to 1989, Dr. C. Everett Koop published reports on the dangers of passive smoking, made warning labels more explicit, worked to restrict sales and distribution of tobacco products to minors, and sought to ban all advertising for cigarettes and tobacco.

They have stressed that the issue is less one of individual rights than of health, and that restrictions may save lives either by compelling people to limit or quit smoking, or by preventing some from starting the habit.

State and local restrictions may not please all lawmakers, but it is highly encouraging to health advocates, who are pressing for ever more stringent regulations. In the 1988 Surgeon General's Report, *The Health Consequences of Smoking: Nicotine*

(continued on p. 99)

WASHINGTON—In her first meeting as head of a federal committee on smoking, Surgeon General Antonia Novello, MD, joined other top health officials in urging states to enforce laws barring cigarette sales to minors.

"The issue of smoking and children is one that concerns me greatly," Dr. Novello said. "If current smoking rates were to continue in the United States, then about 5 million of the children now living in this country would die of smoking-related disease.

Officials Ask States to Bar Cigarette Sales to Minors

"That alarming statistic should be enough to raise this issue to the top of the public agenda."

Dr. Novello's remarks at the May [1990] meeting of the federal Interagency Committee on Smoking and Health echoed those of her boss, Health and Human Services Secretary Louis Sullivan, MD. A week earlier, at a Senate Finance Committee hearing, Dr. Sullivan urged states to adopt a model tobacco-sales-control bill.

The proposed legislation would ban cigarette vending machines and require a special license for merchants to sell tobacco. Merchants could be then fined and their license suspended if they sold to minors.

The interagency committee that Dr. Novello chairs as surgeon general includes officials from more than a dozen federal agencies, plus several private physicians, including AMA trustee Lonnie R. Bristow, MD. It meets several times a year to hear from various interest groups and the public on smoking issues and to exchange information about agency anti-smoking programs.

The May [1990] meeting focused on cigarette sales to children and adolescents. Officials from several anti-smoking groups testified, as did a police officer and a lawyer involved in efforts to curb teen-age smoking.

Bruce R. Talbot, a police officer from Woodridge, Ill., told the committee of his community's experience with a law similar to the bill Dr. Sullivan suggested.

The Woodridge tobacco-license law, put into effect last year, is similar to a liquor license ordinance. A merchant who sells cigarettes to minors is subject to fines of up to $500 and license suspension. Repeat offenders can lose their licenses. The law also has merchants place warning signs near cash registers and install lock-out devices on cigarette vending machines. . . .

During two "sting" operations in the months after the law took effect, several merchants were found still selling cigarettes to minors, Talbot said. The merchants received warnings and were later fined. The latest "sting" showed no such sales, he said.

"But without a national approach to this problem, our efforts will be for naught," said Talbot.

Edward Greer, a lawyer for a public interest anti-smoking group in

Massachusetts, told the committee of a lawsuit, *Kyte v. Philip Morris Inc.*, stemming from cigarette sales to minors. Greer represents two teens who are suing a convenience store and tobacco maker Philip Morris for illegally selling them cigarettes.

Greer said *Kyte* could serve as a test case on whether tobacco makers can be held responsible for such sales.

Forty-four states and the District of Columbia now have tobacco-sales-to-minors laws, but they are rarely enforced, the HHS inspector general said recently.

Retail organizations argue against tobacco-license laws. They say merchants already take steps, such as educating store clerks to sell cigarettes only to adults, to prevent sales to minors.

—Laurie Jones

Source: Laurie Jones, *American Medical News* (15 June 1990), pp. 1, 31.

Did You Know That . . .

There are government restrictions on cigarette advertising in virtually all of the industrialized countries, and labels warning about the health dangers of smoking are now required on cigarette packages worldwide.

Addiction, C. Everett Koop argued that every state government should establish policies restricting the sale and distribution of tobacco products. [15] Koop believes that the distribution of tobacco should be as restricted as that of alcohol. He and other advocates are pressing for state-wide policies limiting the use of vending machines and enforcing bans of the sale of cigarettes to minors.

Although 44 states and the District of Columbia currently ban the sale of cigarettes to those under 18, reports indicate that minors still have an easy time purchasing them. Vending machines in these states simply have a sign stating that the purchase of cigarettes by those under 18 is unlawful, and merchants rarely, if ever, ask their customers for age verifications. According to a recent study at the University of Massachusetts Medical School, 3 million people under the age of 18 purchase 974 million packs of cigarettes each year, and in 1988 the tobacco industry earned $221 million—about 3 percent of their total profit—from sales to minors. [16]

In 1990 Health and Human Services Secretary Louis Sullivan proposed legislation to improve enforcement of state cigarette-sales laws. These laws would 1) Require merchants to buy a license in order to sell cigarettes in the same way restaurants and bars are required to have licenses to sell alcohol. 2) Set specific, graduated penalties for merchants who do violate the sales law. First offenses may bring about a fine, second offenses a larger fine, and third-time offenders would have their licenses sus-

(continued on p. 102)

Achieving a Smoke-Free Society

The health of a new generation could go up in smoke if the institutions dedicated to protecting our country's youth continue to turn their backs on the long-term hazards of tobacco.

Johnny turns 18 this spring. It is a magic time, a coming of age that will mark his graduation from high school and the first time he will be eligible to vote. In New York State, Johnny will also be old enough to buy and smoke cigarettes. Like a lot of other young people, Johnny already smokes. After all, what is the harm? It is not an illicit drug; it is not even alcohol. It is only a cigarette.

ONLY A CIGARETTE?

Our greatest health threat, according to the world's leading medical authorities, is tobacco. In the United States alone, every year an estimated 350,000 to 485,000 smokers fall victim to heart attacks, strokes, lung cancer, chronic bronchitis, and emphysema. By comparison, alcohol kills close to 100,000 people, while all other dependence-producing drugs combined are responsible for some 35,000 deaths annually. These grim statistics point to only one logical goal: To place tobacco at the top of the list in our war against drugs. But, how likely are we to succeed?

Confronted with the ever-growing menace of bad news from the health front and the daily attrition of 1,000 deaths and 4,000 quitters, the tobacco firms have launched advertising and promotional campaigns unparalleled in modern history in volume and motivational wizardry. Specifically, they have aimed at allaying the fears of smokers to keep them smoking, and at enticing youth to secure a new generation of reliable customers. To these ends, the industry has persistently denied that tobacco causes disease, and has adopted a marketing strategy that artfully exploits the perceived needs, wants, and vulnerabilities of the adolescent. Although their ads are allegedly geared to adults, there can be little doubt that they appeal to children. A case in point is Parliament Lights' advertising campaign.

Its headline reads: "The Perfect Recess." At first glance, the headline seems to refer to Parliament's special filter. But the implied message to school children, and to the child in all of us, is plainly obvious.

From the "recess" that can be "perfect" to candy cigarettes, toys, and T-shirts, all embellished with logos of cigarette brands, to the industry-sponsored athletic events and rock concerts, the young are virtually inundated with the seductive imagery of tobacco use to make sure that they will either become active consumers themselves, or at least accept smoking and dipping tobacco as a perfectly natural, normal, even desirable behavior of their peers and elders.

GOVERNMENT APPROVED?

Ninety percent of all smokers begin their habit as children. That's why it is crucial to educate youngsters at home and at school about the dangers of smoking as early as possible. Yet there is no organized nationwide effort dedicated to educating children about the disastrous consequences of tobacco use.

The much publicized "Just Say No" program, which teaches children to stay away from addictive drugs, focuses on drugs and alcohol, with tobacco hardly ever being mentioned. Indeed, "drugs and alcohol" is the ever-present label one encounters when programs, projects, task forces, legislative bodies, treatment centers, or schools deal with substance abuse. It is almost like telling society, "Say NO to drugs and alcohol, but say YES to tobacco."

Even the U.S. Department of Education gets failing grades when it comes to informing students about smoking. In the department's booklet "School Without Drugs," of which 1.5 million copies were distributed to schools nationwide, the former Secretary of Education, William Bennett, states: "The foremost responsibility of any society is to nurture and protect its children." He goes on to say, "Alcohol is an illegal drug for minors and should be treated as such." Tobacco is also an illegal substance for minors, yet the Secretary of Education avoids this and all other issues concerning tobacco. Adding insult to injury, the entire 78-page booklet contains only four brief and innocent references to smoking.

Mr. Bennett's and the Department of Education's nonposition on smoking is puzzling. It ignores a top authority, the U.S. Surgeon General, who reports that tobacco is one of the most addictive substances known to man. Just consider this single fact: a pack-a-day smoker inhales 70,000 puffs a year. Mr. Bennett's head-in-the-sand attitude also failed to consider that tobacco use is recognized by prominent scientific investigators as a "gateway" drug that often opens the doors to the use of illicit substances. The exclusion of tobacco from drug and health educational programs may still have other adverse consequences for both students and teachers. Any message that does not implicate tobacco as a serious health hazard will, in fact, be most persuasive to the younger child whose naive sense of fairness cannot comprehend that the government would permit the sale and promotion of a product "if it were really that bad." This simplistic logic will render children easy prey to the industry's recruiting tactics and usher them more readily into the drug world. As for teachers, tobacco's low profile in drug prevention programs may prevent them from seeking adequate knowledge that should be transmitted to their students.

CONSPIRACY OF SILENCE

An unfortunate reason why tobacco is so low on the nation's list of concern is that, quite simply, it brings in too much tax revenue at every level to expect government to ban or control tobacco marketing, or even to enforce existing restrictions. The profits made by cigarette makers and promoters, and the tax revenues levied by local, state, and federal agencies have united these beneficiaries in a common cause that has given tobacco a clout that is totally unique for a commodity that maims, kills, and, unlike alcohol, is virtually devoid of any socially redeeming value. Regrettably, there is only slim hope that Congress will place the welfare of the people ahead of the financial gain of the tobacco industry. A recent court opinion even cites Congress' "carefully drawn balance between the purposes of warning the public of the hazards of cigarette smoking and protecting the interests of the national economy." This so-called "balance," however, translates into a national death toll of almost a half-million people per year at a monetary loss of $65 billion for health care and lost productivity.

The smoking gun also points at newspapers and magazines that accept cigarette advertisements and suppress information about the dangers of smoking in order to protect their publications' advertising revenue. Harvard epidemiologist John Baylar aptly called "the sharp and continuing rise in deaths from lung cancer, nearly all from cigarette smoking . . . a medical, social and political scandal."

HOPE FOR TOMORROW

In spite of an increasingly powerful tobacco industry, we can help our children achieve a smoke-free society. To start, we must expose the duplicity of the tobacco industry, the government, and the media. All of them ignore or deny the hazards of tobacco while they harvest substantial financial gain. The real cost is not measured in dollars; it is measured in lost lives.

Ideally, a new initiative against tobacco should begin on a national level with full support from the top—the White House. This initiative should deal with tobacco, along with alcohol and drugs of abuse, in an even-handed fashion that is in correct proportion to the damage they inflict. Only then can we hope to achieve a smoke-free—and drug-free—America.

—*Dr. K. H. Ginzel*

Source: K. H. Ginzel, *Priorities* (Summer 1989), pp. 5–7.

FIGURE 5.4
Don't Get Sucked In

Source: American Lung Association.

Many states are considering limiting the use of vending machines and enforcing bans on the sale of cigarettes to minors.

pended. 3) Require all states to post signs declaring that the selling of cigarettes to minors is illegal. 4) Ban cigarette vending machines completely. 5) Rely mainly on civil penalties to avoid tying up the court system.

Needless to say, the passage of this legislation would make it much more difficult for minors to buy cigarettes. It would also be an important victory for those who are pressing for more preventive measures regarding cigarette consumption. Opponents of such laws stress that regardless of policies and regulations, teenagers who want to smoke will, and that restrictive laws serve more as a threat to individual freedom than as a useful method of prevention. But health advocates say that limiting the access minors have to cigarettes may prevent many of them from starting to smoke. Such actions, coupled with planned educational programs, should cut down the number of young people who start smoking each year, an important step toward a smoke-free America by the year 2000.

Kicking the Habit

"QUITTING SMOKING is easy," the American writer Mark Twain once noted. "I've done it hundreds of times." Twain's confession could apply to millions of people who are battling an addiction more powerful than that of heroin, alcohol, or cocaine. Nevertheless, the 1989 Surgeon General's Report announced that more than half of all Americans who had smoked had kicked the habit. [1] The report labeled this achievement "phenomenal," and indeed it is. Heavy smokers who quit are subject to a host of unpleasant side effects, from weight gain and headaches to depression and insomnia. In addition, more than half of those who stop smoking suffer a relapse, and some, like Twain, begin smoking just as heavily as they ever did. With the unpleasant side effects and the low chance of success, why do so many continue the quest for a life without cigarettes?

The answer, no doubt, is that however uncomfortable quitting the habit can be, most people know that the consequences are less terrible than those of cigarettes themselves. They are also heartened by reports that quitting cigarettes can lessen and, eventually, undo completely their chances of suffering the illnesses to which cigarette smoking had made them more vulnerable. As we saw in chapter 3, those who have quit smoking and have been without a cigarette for 5 years or more have as low a chance of suffering lung cancer, heart problems, or COLD (Chronic Obstructive Lung Disease) as those who have never smoked at all.

Moreover, antismoking policies in offices and other public places have forced the issue for many smokers, some of whom are not allowed to smoke on the job at all. Others who are thinking of having children have realized that quitting smoking right away would benefit not only their own health, but that of their unborn child. Parents who stay home to care for their children have learned that subjecting their family to sidestream smoke can cause infection and illness.

Of course, making the decision to quit smoking is only the first step in a serious process that requires complete dedication and commitment. Some smokers are able to put away their pack of cigarettes and quit smoking for good—"cold turkey"—right

(continued on p. 107)

Toward a Smoke-Free Society

If you are one of the 50 million adult Americans who still smoke cigarettes, now is the best time to quit. The incentives to end your affair with nicotine have never been greater.

Nationally, less than three adults in 10 smoke. In many social circles, less than 10 percent of people still smoke, and even fewer dare to smoke in public. And the places where smokers are permitted to light up are growing ever smaller and farther between.

Restrictive legislation and public pressures are increasingly turning smokers into social pariahs who must sneak off by themselves or ask others for permission to smoke. The time is ripe to expedite the goal of the former Surgeon General, C. Everett Koop: to create a smoke-free society by the year 2000.

The economy can no longer afford the 1,000 deaths a day and the even greater number of serious illnesses directly attributable to cigarette smoking. The majority of Americans who are nonsmokers are no longer willing to have their own health jeopardized by the noxious habit of the minority. The evidence that passive smoking is harmful is so convincing that the Environmental Protection Agency now lists it as a serious environmental hazard.

But how can so many people be weaned from cigarettes? Almost every smoker questioned in surveys believes the habit is personally harmful, and more than four smokers in five express a desire to quit. Most have tried one or more times to break their addiction to nicotine; alas, they relapse, usually within a few days or weeks, but sometimes years later. Typically it takes four to 10 attempts before a potential quitter finally makes it stick.

It is certainly not easy—many heavily addicted smokers say quitting was the hardest thing they have ever done, but all who really want to quit can find a way to become former smokers forever. As one exasperated would-be quitter put it: "There are as many ways to quit smoking as there are people who have quit, and I've tried them all! Now, I've got to find the one that was tailor-made for me."

Tales That Inspire

In a fascinating and inspiring book, "The Last Puff" (W. W. Norton), Dr. John W. Farquhar and Dr. Gene A. Spiller give 30 former smokers a chance to share the secrets of their success. The stories can be a source of inspiration, hope and helpful hints for smokers who have, like the storytellers, made repeated failed attempts to quit.

Each found a particular trigger that prompted yet another effort, this time for keeps.

One man, a three-pack-a-day smoker for 30 years, finally quit after his wife agreed to the purchase of a fancy new car if he agreed never to smoke in it. Then, as soon as the car arrived, the couple left on a three-week, crosscountry trip in it.

One woman, a college teacher and writer for whom words and cigarettes were intricately entwined, finally decided to quit for good after seeing a smoker who appeared much older than her years and was beginning to "look like an ashtray" with wrinkled, gray skin, yellow teeth and fingers, and thin, limp hair.

A man who wrote advertising copy for a tobacco company said he quit "because it began to nauseate me that I was a slave to tobacco," adding, "My whole life revolved around being able to smoke." He had to leave concerts, the theater, movies, every 20 to 25 minutes to smoke and even resented sleeping because it meant he couldn't smoke.

What nearly all had in common was a long "incubation period"—usually years of thinking they wanted to get the tobacco monkey off their backs, plus innumerable failed attempts. They also all learned from their earlier failures. They learned what didn't work and, on the final attempt, many tried a new tack.

For Elton W., a public relations specialist, it was a new attitude that spelled success. "In all the previous attempts," he said, "I acted out of a spirit of self-sacrifice. I was giving up something that I liked and quitting was unpleasant. I felt like a martyr."

On his final attempt 20 years ago, he changed his perspective. He practiced a new identity: that of a nonsmoker. He imagined himself in all kinds of situations in which someone might offer a cigarette and then said out loud, "No, thanks, I don't smoke." Not "I'm trying to quit" but "No, I don't smoke." And he imagined himself to be a super-wholesome person, a squeaky clean Goody Two-Shoes, the kind of person no one would dare to offer a cigarette to.

Several successful quitters found it easiest to do on vacation. Being away from familiar surroundings and the usual triggers and stresses that prompt them to reach for a cigarette helped them break the habit.

As for the means to this coveted end, more than 90 percent of the 43 million Americans who have stopped smoking did so on their own. Most of the successful quitters quit cold turkey, some after cutting down or switching to a less potent brand of cigarette but most just by throwing away all their cigarettes and their smoking accouterments.

Challenge for Women

Women have an especially hard time giving up cigarettes. If current trends continue, in five years there will be more American women than men who are smokers. And smoking-related diseases, like lung cancer, are rising among women at astronomical rates. Yet, most research on quitting techniques has focused on men.

To deal with the special problems of women who smoke, like a fear of weight gain if they quit and a strong dependence on cigarettes to cope with stress, Sue Delaney, herself a former smoker who puffed away two packs a day for 40 years, has written a small but very valuable guide, "Women Smokers Can Quit: A Different Approach" (Women's Healthcare Press). The book can be purchased directly by calling 800-543-3854 or by writing to Women's Healthcare Press, 500 Davis Street, Suite 700, Evanston, Ill. 60201.

A surprising number of Americans who have stopped smoking say their physician's advice to quit was the most important motivating factor. Yet only 46 percent of all smokers surveyed last year by the United States Public Health Service said they had been advised by a physician to quit smoking. Even fewer people have been actively counseled as to how to go about quitting.

Doctors can now prescribe a nicotine-containing gum to ease withdrawal. For some smokers, this temporary aid enables them to make a concerted effort to stop smoking and wean themselves from a behavioral dependence on cigarettes without suffering through the extreme irritability of nicotine withdrawal that can prompt family, friends and co-workers to beg them to resume smoking. Smokers who depend heavily on the relaxant and stimulant effects of nicotine can become hooked on the gum, but the gum is easier to give up than cigarettes.

Other aids that help some people include hypnosis (especially when the smoker learns self-hypnosis); acupuncture, which can reduce the craving for addictive drugs, and a variety of relaxation techniques, which can calm the raw nerves of a would-be quitter and provide them with an alternative way to relax.

But this does not mean that organized stop-smoking programs are of little or no use. While it is true that less than 10 percent of former smokers quit through such programs, those who do best in a group setting are nearly always smokers who have repeatedly tried to quit on their own and failed. Success is fostered by group support, the feeling that they are not the only ones going through this, the helpful hints offered by the counselor and other participants and in many cases the fact that they paid for the program.

And even when a relapse occurs after completing an organized program, the learning experience can often abet success of a future effort to quit on one's own.

The bottom line of stop-smoking efforts, then, is the old Boy Scout motto: If at first you don't succeed, try, try again, because each failure can be a steppingstone to future success. And by the year 2000 the air both outside and inside the lungs of Americans can be a lot cleaner.

Source: Jane Brody, "Personal Health," *New York Times*, 12 July 1990, sec. 2, p. 8.

away. Others need more assistance. For those people an entire industry exists. Independent self-help groups can provide literature offering advice to hopeful smokers trying to quit. Physicians and psychiatrists can offer therapies such as **acupuncture, hypnotism**, even **laser therapy** to deaden one's desire for nicotine. Hospitals have inpatient programs that treat the smoker much like a drug addict, calling for total abstinence immediately. Both the United States and Canada have many group programs that help participants set and stick to a realistic program in which they will cut down on—and eventually quit—the habit. The success of these programs is certainly not guaranteed. It depends to a great extent on the participant's nature and willpower. Every smoker who wants to quit must make a definite commitment to this goal in order to be successful.

GOING SOLO

Many smokers who have decided to quit proceed in their own way and at their own pace rather than seeking professional help or joining some sort of group program. A very substantial number of them succeed. Of the 43 million smokers who have quit during the past 25 years, about 90 percent have succeeded without help from organized groups or from devices and treatments that promise to make the quitting process easier. [2] Some of these people have simply rid themselves of any remaining cigarettes,

Acupuncture: Chinese system of inserting needles at various "pressure points" on the body; unproven as a smoking-cessation device.

Hypnotism: The act of inducing sleep or a form of meditation; has had moderate success as a smoking-cessation device.

Laser therapy: The use of a laser beam, which is a device that produces a concentrated beam of light radiation, for certain medical procedures.

FIGURE 6.1
Trends in Smoking

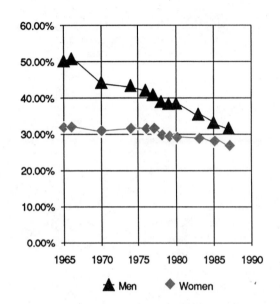

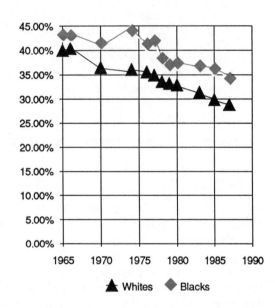

Source: Office on Smoking and Health, Centers for Disease Control.

Smoking has decreased significantly since the mid-60s when the first public warnings were issued by the Surgeon General's office.

thrown away ashtrays, lighters, and other smoking accessories, and quit smoking then and there for good.

Others decide to phase out their smoking gradually. Some do this by allowing themselves a daily quota of cigarettes and reducing this quota weekly until it reaches zero. Others do it by systematically lengthening the period between cigarettes or by resisting the urge to smoke as long as possible, so that the number of cigarettes smoked each day diminishes. Quitting on one's own has a number of advantages. To begin with, it costs nothing. Perhaps more important, smokers can tailor their quitting process to their own style of life and daily routine without spending time and money on group meetings.

Improving Your Chances

When you stop smoking, you automatically reduce your chances of dying from a smoking-related disease. The longer you abstain, the less likely you are to succumb, until after about fifteen years of nonsmoking your chances of unnecessary early death are just about the same as for someone who has never smoked. How long you smoked makes little difference to the general trend, so it is *always* worth giving up. The graph [below] shows how the average smoker's chances of dying from lung cancer (compared to a nonsmoker) decrease from the time he or she stops smoking. This tendency, though less marked than for lung cancer, applies to all the illnesses associated with smoking.

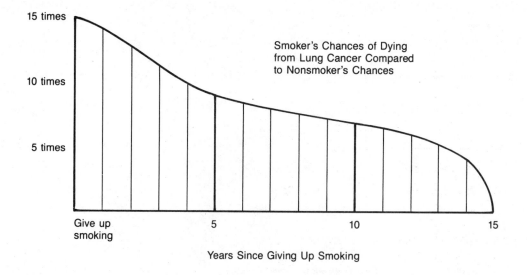

Smoker's Chances of Dying from Lung Cancer Compared to Nonsmoker's Chances

Years Since Giving Up Smoking

Source: Kunz and Finkel, eds., *The AMA Family Medical Guide* (New York: Random House, 1987), p. 42.

On the other hand, quitting alone places the entire burden on the individual and does not provide him or her with support or sympathy from others who share the same struggle. And, of course, if there is a relapse, fewer people will know about it and provide encouragement to try again. Because there are no set rules to follow except for the person's own, there are also no tried-and-accepted ways to deal with a relapse. This can be very hard on the participant, who has to fight feelings of frustration and discouragement virtually by himself or herself.

FIGURE 6.2
Smoking Alternatives

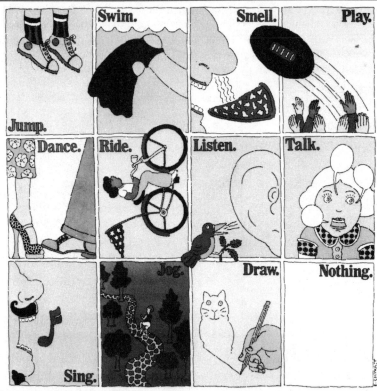

Source: American Cancer Society.

When tempted to smoke, try one of these alternative activities suggested by the American Cancer Society instead of lighting a cigarette.

Group participation programs: Programs designed to help several people quit smoking through the help of regularly scheduled meetings.

Independent quitting programs: Programs that provide literature, videos, and other information designed to help a smoker quit.

SELF-HELP PROGRAMS

Self-help groups are divided into two subsets: **group participation programs** and **independent quitting programs**. The latter provide literature and other materials designed to help a smoker quit. One program, Freedom From Smoking, is an American Lung Association-sponsored package that provides two self-help manuals for smokers intending to quit. The first of these pamphlets, entitled *Freedom from Smoking in 20 Days*, offers day-to-

(continued on p. 112)

Whether you quit smoking gradually or go cold turkey, there are lots of tricks you can use to get yourself through the difficult times. Try some or all of these hints for success. If one doesn't work, another might.

★ Choose a quit date, and stick to it. This is the most important step in any stop-smoking program.

★ Remember that if you are addicted to nicotine, the first few days off cigarettes will be the hardest.

Hints for Success

★ Write down your most important reason for quitting. Keep it with you, so that you can look at it when you have the urge to smoke.

★ Change the habits which accompany smoking. For instance, if you always have a cigarette with coffee in the morning, drink orange juice instead of coffee.

★ Tell everyone you're quitting and ask your friends to help you stay off cigarettes.

★ Keep a supply of sugarless gum, celery sticks, cinnamon sticks, or hard peppermints on hand to use as a smoking substitute.

★ When the urge to smoke strikes—wait. You'll find that the craving for a cigarette will often pass in just a few minutes. Within a week or two, cravings will have disappeared completely.

★ Drink lots of water.

★ Never carry matches or a lighter with you.

★ Bet with someone that you can quit. Put the money you would spend on cigarettes in a jar each day. If you smoke, you pay your friend the money. You keep the money if you don't smoke by the end of the week.

★ Put away your ashtrays or fill them with something else like walnuts, coins or flowers.

★ Brush your teeth a lot to get rid of the taste of tobacco.

★ If you have an uncontrollable urge to light up, take ten deep breaths instead. Hold the last breath, then exhale slowly and tell yourself you've just *had* a cigarette. Now it's time to do something else!

★ Eat three small meals a day instead of one or two large ones. This maintains blood sugar levels and decreases the urge to smoke.

★ Spend time with people who don't smoke or who are trying to quit.

★ To cope with tension, try this deep breathing exercise. Stand with your feet apart and comfortable. Close your eyes and slowly let your head fall forward. Breathe in through your nose, and slowly let your head rise as your lungs fill up with air. Hold it for a moment, and then slowly exhale through your nose. Take more time exhaling than inhaling. Repeat.

Source: *Breaking Free* (New York: American Cancer Society, 1986), p. 9.

Surveys indicate that nearly 90 percent of all smokers wish they could give up smoking.

day activities to help the smoker reach that goal. The second manual, *A Lifetime of Freedom from Smoking,* helps the former smoker remain free from cigarettes permanently.

Another company, Health Innovations, Inc., has marketed a computerized device called LifeSign, which contains a display panel with two windows. Based on information the participant has fed into its memory, the credit-card-sized device displays in one of its windows the amount of hours its owner must wait before smoking a cigarette and in the other the number of days until he or she must quit the habit completely. The participant must push a button on the machine every time he or she lights a cigarette. If the designed schedule is violated, a buzzer sounds. Health Innovations has sold more than half a million LifeSign devices, which have shown a marginal success. According to surveys, 25 percent of those who quit smoking with the aid of these computers were still nonsmokers one year after kicking the habit. [3]

GROUP-PARTICIPATION PROGRAMS

In contrast to independent self-help programs, which provide helpful material but leave much of the action up to the participant, group-participation programs meet regularly and are designed to help several people stop smoking at the same time. Some of these groups feature a panel of former smokers who explain how they were able to kick the habit successfully. Others take a behavior-modification approach. During meetings participants discuss the rituals they associate with smoking. Some enjoy a cigarette after breakfast, for example, or with a cup of coffee. Changing these types of patterns—by having breakfast at the office if smoking is restricted there or by skipping the morning coffee—may help lessen the temptation to smoke.

Another program, Smoker's Anonymous, has borrowed its approach from the 12-step program initiated by **Alcoholics Anonymous**. In regularly scheduled meetings, participants announce to a roomful of fellow smokers that they are powerless over nicotine. Through sponsors (each new participant is assigned a sponsor, a fellow member who offers sympathy and moral support) and constant meetings, participants learn to live their lives without depending on cigarettes.

As with all of the 12-step programs, Smoker's Anonymous does not cost anything and stresses total and immediate abstinence as the only effective way to quit the habit successfully.

Alcoholics Anonymous (AA): An organization founded by two alcoholics in the 1930s; dedicated to helping others fight alcohol addiction through regular meetings and a specific 12-step program.

(continued on p. 114)

Did You Know That . . .

Approximately 43 million Americans have quit smoking since 1964.

"You told us we could bring all the cigarettes we wanted!" cries a red-faced man. "This is *ridiculous!* This is false advertising! How can I get out of this?" All around, jaws are working. The air holds the sound of clicking gum, the phlegmy rattle of smoker's cough.

Barbara Davidson, a psychiatric social worker, stands at the front of the room at the Sheraton City Squire, smiling down on 27 people. Each has paid $295 for six weekly meetings of SmokEnders, an organization that promises to help people break the habit. Davidson tells the red-faced man that the room is too small for smoking, and besides, a city ordinance soon to take effect will ban smoking at public gatherings. But she promises that people can smoke in the hallway during breaks. What's more, she assures them, they can keep on smoking at work, at home, wherever the law allows—until their cutoff date in three weeks. "*I* quit smoking on January 3, 1973," says Davidson. "Every morning when I woke up, I took two or three drags just to get my heart started. . . . Now, how are *you* feeling tonight? Tell me what's happening."

Up in Smoke

"I feel like I'm in grammar school," says one woman.

"I'm afraid of the physical effects of withdrawal," says another.

Davidson assures the group that they'll be detoxified slowly, that by the time they quit completely they'll suffer only a "mild jolt." Soon she turns cheerleader. "Learn to love yourself," she says. "And use *hate* against cigarettes and your smoking habit."

A million or so smokers live in the New York area, and the U.S. Public Health Service claims that 90 percent of them say they'd like to stop. That figure may get higher as laws and rules increasingly close the worlds open to smokers. Treatments for the habit, from hypnotism to counseling, continue to spring up. SmokEnders, whose nineteen-year-old program relies on positive-reinforcement and group-therapy techniques, claims that 84 percent of its graduates still aren't smoking after a year.

"Take out your binders," Davidson tells her class. The 27 smokers reach for the packets they've been given. Inside are stickers, labels, poems, logbooks, and charts—morale boosters and little projects designed to keep hands busy and away from cigarettes. There is an "oral-gratification kit"—a pack containing dental floss, toothpaste, a toothbrush, mouthwash—and a green paper strap to be wrapped around a cigarette pack. On it, the smokers are to record the number of cigarettes they consume per hour.

Davidson tells the group to jot in their logbooks, "I will stop smoking . . . on Thursday, March 17, 1988."

"Omigod!" gasps a woman.

"That is going to be the most wonderful day of your life," says Davidson.

The class goes on for an hour, and the audience begins to stir. Sixty minutes of nicotine deprivation! Davidson starts talking fast. She quotes William James: "The greatest discovery of my generation is that human beings can alter their lives by altering their attitudes of mind." Then she moves to *The Little Engine That Could:* "I think I can, I think I can." She tells her students to calculate how much they would save by stopping: Two-pack-a-day smokers, paying $1.20 a pack, could net $876 a year.

At last she says, "You seem like a smart group—you're catching on fast. . . . I know you guys are really dying to get up and stretch."

The class bolts for the hall. Soon the air is clogged with smoke. "That room is *too* small," gripes one woman. The red-faced man gathers up his coat and leaves for good.

Ten minutes later, Davidson gives out the assignments for next week. "Plan a wonderful reward to enjoy on March 17. Go to the theater. . . . If you hate your job, *quit* it." She tells the class to smoke as many cigarettes as they like for the next week but to change brands.

"I smoke two different brands," a woman in blue cashmere says. "Can I use the other one?"

"No!"

"If I smoke Kent Golden Lights, can I just change to another Kent?"

"*No!*"

Davidson talks about coping with the "need for mouthiness," that craving to have something in your mouth. "Brush your teeth long and lovingly," she says. "Sex up your wisdom teeth! Say 'hi' to your molars!"

In the back, a man leaves to smoke a cigarette.

"Now," says Davidson, "recite all together: I *will* stop smoking."

"I *will* stop smoking."

"I *will* feel better."

"I *will* feel better."

"I *will* look better."

"I *will* look better."

"*I will* be *free!*"

—*Dinitia Smith*

Source: Dinitia Smith, *New York* (18 April 1988), p. 75.

Withdrawal: The physiological and/or psychological effects of discontinued use of a drug.

Behavior modification: The application of certain conditioning techniques to modify or control behavior.

Other groups call for a slower **withdrawal**. SmokEnders, which has been helping smokers since 1968, [4] takes this approach. During the first four weeks of its six-week program, participants are allowed to smoke but are encouraged to cut down as much as they can. In the meantime, they strive through **behavior modification** to lessen the urge they have for a cigarette. In the last two weeks of the program participants are not supposed to smoke. During this time the program will help them cope in healthier ways with situations and emotions that once would have compelled them to smoke. SmokEnders costs about $295 for a six-week seminar.

Both Smoker's Anonymous and SmokEnders have about a 25 percent success rate. That percentage may seem low, but most self-help groups have similar numbers. Indeed, most experts advise those who want to stop smoking to try to do so on their own, not only once but twice or three times, before trying either an independent or a group-participation program. The most desperate smokers, those whose habit exceeds a pack a day, have a serious addiction that may call for outside help. In fact, part of the reason more people quit smoking successfully when they do so on their own is that light smokers almost always are able to quit without assistance. Therefore, a higher percentage of smokers who seek outside help are those who have a more serious addiction. In addition, the percentage may be a bit misleading; people who fail the first time they complete a quit-smoking program may succeed the second or third time they enter such a program.

NICOTINE-CONTAINING SUBSTITUTES

Independent and group-participation programs can be effective ways of dealing with the psychological aspects of quitting smoking, but heavy smokers may require more help kicking their habit. They are, after all, physically addicted to nicotine and may have to continue to take diminishing dosages of the drug in order to break their dependence. This concept is similar to that behind **methadone**, a synthetic narcotic that heroin addicts have taken while withdrawing from heroin. Methadone has met with some degree of success in clinics across the country. Inspired by this, Merrel Dow Pharmaceuticals, Inc., received authorization from the U.S. Food and Drug Administration in 1984 to market Nicorette, a gum containing nicotine (Nicorette is a brand name for nicotine polacrilex gum), in the United States.

Nicorette contains nicotine bound to an ion exchange resin; when chewed, the gum releases small amounts of nicotine, which the lining of the mouth absorbs. This action produces blood levels of nicotine that help reduce the withdrawal symptoms many people experience when they stop smoking cigarettes.

Once the first hurdle has been overcome, withdrawing from nicotine becomes easier. First, because a person receives a smaller amount of nicotine at a slower rate from the gum than

Methadone: A synthetic narcotic, less powerful than heroin, often prescribed for the relief of pain and as a temporary therapy for recovering morphine and heroin addicts.

from a cigarette, the dosage of the drug is not as intense or as pleasurable from Nicorettes. Second, receiving nicotine from gum rather than a cigarette denies the user a certain amount of pleasure. Many people are as addicted to the ritual of lighting a cigarette and drawing on it as they are to the nicotine the cigarette contains.

Nicorette is available in boxes containing 96 pieces of gum and costs about $30 a package. Each piece of gum contains two milligrams of nicotine. Most smokers use 8 to 10 pieces of gum each day over a period of 8 to 12 weeks. Nicorette is not intended to be a long-term substitute for cigarettes, but a temporary bridge that helps a nicotine addict withdraw from the drug slowly.

Studies show that Nicorette can be an effective method if used correctly. Initial reports done in 1984 had shown that those who used Nicorette in conjunction with a group-participation program had a long-term success rate that was twice as high as the rates for patients participating in the same programs who used **placebo** gum. [5] In a follow-up study, Danish investigators recently conducted a study of 173 adults who were participating in a stop-smoking program that combined gum with counseling. The study concluded that participants who chewed gum containing nicotine had more success quitting smoking than those who chewed placebo gum. [6]

Later reports concurred with these original studies but also found that if not used in conjunction with a quit-smoking program, Nicorette was often ineffective or, even worse, a substitute addiction. One of the problems clinics distributing methadone to heroin addicts found was that those who used to be dependent on the stronger opiate had merely switched dependencies and had become hooked on the substance designed to help them become drug-free. Surveys done in 1988 and 1989 found the same thing happening among many smokers who were using Nicorette without proper counseling. Instead of smoking a pack of cigarettes a day, users were chewing 15 pieces of gum. [7]

Researchers also found that many physicians were unaware that Nicorette should be used in conjunction with a quit-smoking program and were prescribing the drug to their patients as a sole means of helping them quit smoking. [8] The same studies noted that even if used incorrectly and addictively, Nicorette was a safer alternative to cigarettes. The gum contains lower dosages of nicotine and fewer other hazardous substances than do cigarettes, and, because they are not smoked, they do not damage the respiratory system.

Since the advent of Nicorette scientists have continued to

Placebo: A substance of no physiological therapeutic value; sometimes prescribed for the psychological relief it may offer the patient.

FIGURE 6.3
Nicotine Gum and Blood-Nicotine Levels

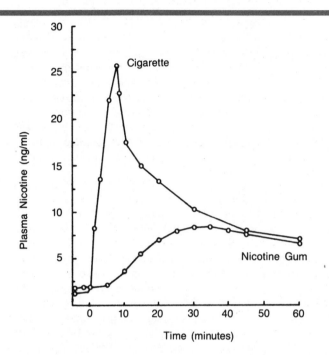

Source: M. A. H. Russell, M. J. Jarvis, and C. Feyerabend, *Lancet,* Vol. 2 (14 December 1985), p. 1370.

This figure compares levels of nicotine in the blood resulting from the consumption of either one piece of nicotine gum or one cigarette per hour. The nicotine gum provides a lower, slower-acting dose of nicotine.

develop nicotine-containing substances as temporary substitutes for cigarettes. One of these is the nicotine patch worn behind the ear. The patch releases small doses of nicotine that are absorbed by the skin in much the same way that Nicorette is absorbed by the skin of the mouth. Researchers are also studying the effects of a nicotine-containing nasal spray. The spray administers a dose of nicotine to the brain at a much quicker rate than either Nicorette or the nicotine patch, so that the smoker will not miss the rush of nicotine that cigarettes supply. In addition, scientists are working with a drug called **clonidine**, which has been used to treat alcohol and opiate dependencies.

In one study done in 1988, doctors at the New York State

(continued on p. 121)

Did You Know That . . .

Researchers advise people to wait at least 15 minutes after eating before using nicotine gum. The acid in many foods and beverages interferes with the absorption of nicotine.

Clonidine: A drug used to treat high blood pressure.

The Art of Quitting Smoking

The face is familiar, but you probably don't know the name: Dave Goerlitz. He's the macho smoker you've seen in the Winston advertisements. But he's not smoking anymore. Not in real life, anyway.

After 24 years of smoking cigarettes, Goerlitz quit a three-pack-a-day habit cold turkey November 17 [1988], the day of the Great American Smokeout. The clincher was not the quit-smoking literature his mother had been bombarding him with. It was the grim sight of lung-cancer patients bedridden in the hospital where he visited his brother.

Not everybody needs a shock to kick the habit. Still, even with real determination and the right tactics, few make it on the first try. The heavier your habit, the longer it is likely to take. Successful quitters take an average of seven years and three to four serious attempts to make the reform stick.

You think you're a lost cause because you've tried and slipped? Maybe you need a new strategy. Unhooking is a matter of matching up with a strategy that works for you. Help abounds, ranging from myriad self-help materials to programs that are loosely organized or formally structured and that cost nothing to hundreds of dollars.

An intensive six-day quit-smoking program, including aerobics and yoga, cost William J. Bennett, the Bush administration's drug "czar," $875 at a West Virginia resort. It's too soon to say for certain whether or not he has permanently kicked a two-pack-a-day habit that stretches back for 20 years. But even if this treatment works for him, there are plenty of inexpensive ways to quit that can be just as effective.

Ex-smokers share two main qualities. Says Ellen Gritz, director of the Division of Cancer Control at UCLA's Johnson Comprehensive Cancer Center: "Motivation to stop and confidence that you will succeed are the most important factors for successful quitting."

And if you still need prodding, the bad news about health and cigarettes has grown worse.

Twenty-five years after the surgeon general's report first declared cigarettes dangerous, the latest report blames smoking for more than one of every six deaths in the U.S. Among women, smoking is the cause of more deaths than breast cancer. Recent studies found that smoking can cause strokes and that smokers' risk of dying from cancer, heart disease or emphysema is much higher than previously thought. In the case of lung cancer alone, the average male smoker is 22 times more likely to die from the disease than a nonsmoker.

Many people find motivation comes easier when the boss makes it harder to smoke at work. For 30 years Al Ledenican smoked, reaching a two-pack-a-day habit without ever trying to quit. That was until his company, Eveready Battery in Westlake, Ohio, declared its building smoke-free. Traipsing to the cafeteria—the only smoking zone—for each cigarette was a chore, so he decided to quit. He broke the habit by following tips from an American Lung Association counselor brought in by the company. Says Ledenican: "I probably wouldn't have done it if the company hadn't taken the initiative."

TRYING THE IMPROMPTU

Make at least one or two serious attempts to stop cold turkey on your own before you plunge into a rigorous plan or formal program. "Most people stop smoking by trial and error, learning from each attempt and figuring out under what conditions relapse occurs," says the University of Rhode Island's Jim Prochaska, a professor of psychology and director of its Self-Change Laboratory, which studies smoking-cessation techniques.

Don't rely on willpower alone. You will do better following a few basic tips.

• Use each cigarette as a chance to solve a problem. When you light up, ask yourself why. To relax? Cool off anger? Socialize? Get going in the morning? Ease boredom? Pure habit? Knowing the reasons why you smoke should help you find alternative coping mechanisms.

• List what you like about smoking. You'll need to find substitutes—perhaps another way to relax after dinner or another object to hold in your hand at parties. Also list your fears and dislikes about smoking. The more negatives you come up with, the more you'll be motivated to stop.

• Arm yourself with tips from the experts. *Clearing the Air,* a guide full of good hints, is available free from the National Cancer Institute by calling 800-4CANCER. An information specialist is on hand to answer any questions you might have. Local chapters of the American Lung Association, American Cancer Society and American Heart Association also offer booklets with helpful quit-smoking tips.

• Set a goal of at least three months to stay off tobacco. Once you have quit for that long, you'll have a better chance of quitting for good.

• Stay upbeat if you relapse. Try to figure out why it happened, then try again. Two-thirds of relapses are in response to boredom, anxiety, depression, anger or other negative feelings, according to Prochaska.

Even the heaviest smokers sometimes succeed with an impromptu approach. But chances are you will need outside help if you smoke more than two packs a day—the badge of heavy smoking—or if you've made more than three or four serious attempts to quit.

GOING SMOKELESS WITH HELP

Quitting may require professional help. "There are no magic bullets. Behavior modification is the primary key," observes UCLA's Gritz, who suggests starting with the least costly and handiest help, no matter how heavy a smoker you are.

SELF-HELP PROGRAMS. With behavior-modification materials you can use on your own, you get the benefit of professional advice without shelling out fees for face-to-face service. Among the better efforts by qualified experts is *Freedom From Smoking for You and Your Family* (American Lung Association), a workbook with easy-to-follow quitting suggestions.

THE GROUP APPROACH. This could be for you if you feel the need for emotional support from others in the same boat. It can also expose you to the right role model. Take Herb Golterman, a 33-year-old St. Louis construction subcontractor who tried everything from pure willpower to nicotine gum and hypnotism. After 15 years, his persistence paid off: He kicked his two-pack-a-day habit in a group behavior-modification program.

Golterman credits a panel of successful former smokers who explained to his American Lung Association group just how they had quit. "I saw that it could be done and vowed that I would be on a panel like that someday," says Golterman. He has since appeared on five such panels.

Group programs typically consist of 25 or fewer would-be quitters, who meet for an hour or two once a week over several weeks. The American Lung Association's program, for example, runs for about eight sessions and costs $35 to $150, depending on the organization that sponsors it. For a list of group programs near you, telephone 800-4CANCER.

Going with a group to kick the smoking habit will usually be cheapest in one of the "volunteer" programs sponsored by the American Lung Association, American Cancer Society or Seventh Day Adventist Church. Call these organizations for details on their programs, often held in community or medical centers.

Such volunteer efforts are on a par with professional programs found elsewhere. But their effectiveness depends on the leader—usually an ex-smoker, not a trained professional. "Frankly, quality varies from terrible to excellent," says Gritz.

If you prefer group help under a trained professional, try a stop-smoking clinic at a college, hospital or medical center. Psychologists or medical doctors run the sessions, often using programs developed by the American Lung Association or Cancer Society. Cost ranges from very little to several hundred dollars.

For-profit commercial programs, which have been on the wane since the 1970s, are the costliest. The most widely available one, Smok-Enders, is offered mostly through hospitals and companies as an employee benefit. When it is offered directly to the public, the six-week program costs $295.

How successful are commercial programs? There's no evidence that they work better or worse than lower-cost programs. In an evaluation by the National Cancer Institute, one Smok-Enders program had a success rate of about 40% after a year, but another rated only 27% after four years.

THE NICOTINE SUBSTITUTE. The more you smoke and the more addicted you are, the more likely you'll benefit from Nicorette, a prescription chewing gum containing nicotine. Nicorette is far more effective when behavioral counseling is part of the treatment. "Without behavior modification, Nicorette can compound your sense of failure," warns Joan Falk, a clinical psychologist in Chicago.

A . . . study reported in the *Journal of the American Medical Association* says 99.5% of smokers receiving Nicorette prescriptions are not in behavioral programs, even though this is how the FDA stipulates that the gum be used. The study confirmed earlier findings that using Nicorette improperly often results in failure.

A conscientious physician or dentist who prescribes Nicorette might offer limited counseling or steer you to a program. But chances are you'll have to search out your own self-help materials, group program or counseling to supplement the gum.

One good source, *How to Use Nicotine Gum & Other Strategies to Quit Smoking,* by Nina Schneider (Pocket Books), gives useful details on how the gum works and helpful suggestions on altering your behavior to make smoking less attractive. Nicorette typically costs less than $30 for a box of 96 sticks—about $3.60 a day for the minimum effective dose.

Researchers are testing various other drugs, but so far only Nicorette is FDA-approved. Ask your doctor before trying any new remedies.

OTHER WAYS TO GIVE IT UP

Hypnosis may seem like a magic cure, but it is really just an aid for smokers who respond well to suggestion. As with Nicorette, you should combine hypnosis with behavior modification. Most hypnotists provide behavioral counseling as part of their treatment.

Success depends largely on your motivation and the skill and experience of the hypnotist. Look for a licensed mental-health professional with training in hypnosis. For referrals, call a nearby medical school, university or local chapter of the American Society of Clinical Hypnosis.

The acupuncture technique of using a needle or staple device on the ear or pressing a needle to various points on the nose or wrist has its advocates. However, concludes a National Cancer Institute review, "it has not been demonstrated that acupuncture is able to promote smoking cessation. Acupuncture may act as a 'placebo procedure' to help the smoker to handle the addictive component of smoking.

For some people, smoking is clearly tied up with other emotional difficulties. If smoking is your outlet for anger, for example, you'll need another way to blow off steam. A psychologist or psychiatrist would probably have the best training to help you. Only a few concentrate on smoking cessation, so instead of limiting your quest to a smoking-cessation specialist, look for a therapist with experience in helping people overcome addictive behavior.

Start with university psychology departments and medical-school-affiliated hospitals that have psychiatric training programs. They can often provide referrals to therapists through their psychotherapy clinics.

Psychiatrists tend to charge more than psychologists, though fees of either will likely be at least $60 a session and could run $100 or more. Most health insurance policies cover psychotherapy and often reimburse at least 50% of the fee.

—*Nancy Henderson*

Source: Nancy Henderson, *Changing Times* (October 1989), pp. 105–108.

Psychiatric Institute gave clonidine to 71 heavy smokers participating in a behavior modification program and a placebo to
another group participating in the same program. A comparison
of the two groups found that twice as many smokers given
clonidine were able to quit as those who had taken the placebo. [9]
Still on the horizon are therapies that can block the central
effects of nicotine on the brain and drugs that make cigarettes
taste foul.

OTHER OPTIONS

There are still more choices for people hoping to quit smoking.
Several hospitals have added departments in their substance-
abuse programs that deal with nicotine addiction. An example of
this is the Glenbeigh Hospital program in Hialeah, Florida. This
is a 12-day, cold-turkey approach. Participants' cigarettes are
confiscated immediately, and patients are allowed no psychoactive substances whatsoever—including caffeine and sugar. The
philosophy behind this is that virtually all psychoactive substances can cause a craving for nicotine. Each day all participants
go through exercise training and receive special guidance designed to help them face life without cigarettes. The program
staff works closely with the participants and includes a psychiatrist, nutritionist, cardiologist, and a group therapist. The cost of
the program is high—$3,500 for a 12-day session [10], but the
program seems to work for those who have joined it.

Other people are turning to hypnotism or acupuncture to
help them quit smoking. Hypnosis is a focused state of attention
during which the patient is more open to following suggestions
that can change his or her behavior. The hypnotist may suggest,
for example, that the person will achieve a relaxed state of
pleasure through breathing deeply instead of smoking. The next
time the patient craves a cigarette, he or she can substitute a
deep-breathing exercise and get the same effect that previously
came only from the ritual of smoking. Many psychologists and
physicians have received specific training in hypnotism, and
some doctors report that two out of three patients who underwent
hypnotism to help them quit smoking had not resumed the habit
a year later. [11]

Acupuncture is a 3,000-year-old Chinese therapy that involves the insertion of needles into specific pressure points on the
body. The theory behind this practice is that the human body has
a natural balance to it that drugs such as nicotine disrupt. To

FIGURE 6.4
Acupuncture Treatment for Cigarette Addiction

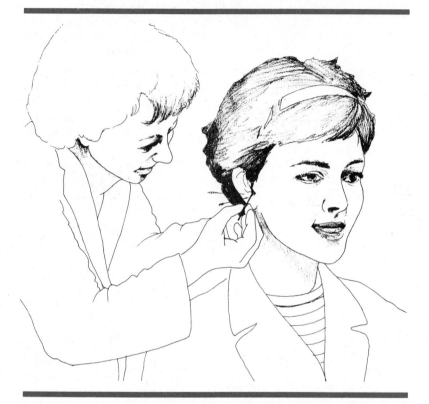

Acupuncture has helped some people reduce their desire for cigarettes. Proponents have suggested that inserting acupuncture needles into specific pressure points in the ears and hands releases endorphins, which help to eliminate the craving for nicotine. Most experts, however, are skeptical of its value.

help a person quit smoking, the acupuncturist will insert needles in the patient's earlobes and hands. A similar practice is laser therapy, in which a medical technician will stimulate those same pressure points with laser beams. Proponents of both acupuncture and laser therapy claim that stimulating those pressure points induces the release of endorphins and thus relieves the craving for nicotine. Both therapies have had mixed success treating smokers, but many experts caution that neither practice is a proven treatment, and both should be approached with skepticism.

GETTING STARTED: A PLAN OF ACTION

So you have decided to quit smoking. What's your first step? Again, most experts recommend that every person who wants to quit should try to do so on his or her own before going for outside help. Cold turkey is one way to do this. Tapering off your habit slowly is another. To do this, choose a date by which you will have quit smoking. You may want to give yourself as long as three months to taper your habit, but keep to the schedule. Record the number of cigarettes you smoke each day and make the number each day less than the day before. By the time your quit-date rolls around, you may find that stopping smoking completely is not as hard as you thought it would be.

If you can't quit on your own—and depending on how heavy your smoking habit is, you may need some assistance—make a

(continued on p. 125)

Knowing When It's Time to Give Up an Unsociable Habit

I have been a smoker, on and off, for almost 40 years and a nonsmoker, on and off, for one. So I feel qualified to make some general unscientific observations and some purely subjective remarks on the subject.

First, let me warn those who persist in their dirty little habit to be prepared to become pariahs as stubborn practitioners of the vile habit who knowingly spread death and disease to mankind.

All because you have been unable or unwilling to try to overcome your longstanding addiction to nicotine.

Forget that it was only a few short years ago that you enjoyed with impunity the company of other addicts all happily smoking their cigarettes and blissfully unaware of the consequences of what they were doing.

This problem and the solution or resolution of it invades nearly every area of our lives. The workplace seems to be the first place headed toward a smoke-free status. Since most of us work in the company of others, it seems right that the majority rules in this case.

In the office where I work, there are 5 smokers among 15 people. We have been told that after April 1, either by company directive or state regulation, there will be no smoking except in designated areas.

Restaurants, which are supposed to offer nonsmoking areas, seldom do, at least not in this part of the country. Consequently, each table more or less makes up its own rules.

I recently enjoyed an evening out with six other women. Our table was a fairly representative group, with one unrepentant smoker, two nonsmokers and four ex-smokers—one of whom now says she is allergic to smoke and one so recently on the wagon that she carried an unopened pack of cigarettes in case of emergency.

After several turns of musical chairs, we settled on a seating arrangement that allowed the smoker to be seated at the end of the table farthest from the ex-smoker who is allergic to smoke, while the newest ex-smoker sat downwind from the smoker so that she could enjoy the aroma from the cigarettes. Thus arranged, we enjoyed dinner.

Smoking in planes is apparently on the way out. Those tiny ashtrays were always a little tough to hit anyway. It does seem that anyone can live without a cigarette for two hours, but let's give the smoker a break on long flights. It would be pretty hard to go cold turkey at 40,000 feet.

The smoking issue even affects the making of ordinary social plans. It is difficult for a nonsmoking couple, especially if they are still in "withdrawal," to spend hours across the bridge table or to share a leisurely meal in a restaurant with active smokers. It is better to wait to see them when all desire to smoke is gone—if you're still friends by then.

Once the decision to quit smoking is made, visits to your nonsmoking friends and family will be much smoother. No longer will your hosts have to search the cupboards for ashtrays, nor will you feel that you should leave the room to light up.

My father, whose good opinion I value, lives in a smoke-free house. I can recall, on a cool April evening, voluntarily going out onto his 10th-floor balcony overlooking downtown Washington to have my after-dinner smoke. At that point, my craving for a cigarette was stronger than my fear of height.

Giving up cigarettes has got to be one of the most difficult things to do. Mature, intelligent people play games with themselves and indulge in self-deceptive practices that would be funny if they weren't so sad.

One of the first schemes that people try is simply to cut down on consumption. You decide not to buy cartons, only an occasional pack, on the theory that you will thereby smoke less. Of course, that doesn't work; you just go to the store more often.

The next idea is to set a limit for yourself; you just need a little self-discipline. Five cigarettes a day seems reasonable: one with morning coffee, one at coffee break, one after lunch, one before dinner and one after dinner. That doesn't work because you forget the one you can't sleep without, the last one before bedtime. You borrow from the next day's ration and that scheme goes down the tubes.

One of the last-ditch efforts is to stop buying cigarettes altogether and to cadge them from your family and friends. This ploy doesn't work, either, and it serves only to alienate people.

So you are back to buying one pack every other day or maybe just smoking on weekends, as my husband and I did. That may work for a while, until the day you run out and it's not your day to buy and you find yourself rummaging through drawers and pocketbooks hoping to find a forgotten pack.

Or you suffer the worst and final humiliation—looking in ashtrays for a long butt. This is hitting bottom. This is the point at which you confront yourself, grow up, fish or cut bait, or some less elegant phrase.

The long and short of it is this: The Surgeon General's report won't do it, the messages on the pack won't do it, no grisly shot of blackened lungs on television will do it (that could never happen to you, you think). You have to decide not that you want to do it, but that you must do it.

Expect to suffer and, in a very real sense, to mourn the loss of a great comfort and pleasure. Don't do it because you've been told how much better your food will taste. Food probably always tasted great anyway.

Don't do it because your wrinkles will disappear. They probably will, plumped out with those pounds that you almost inevitably will put on. Don't do it because people have told you how wonderful you'll feel. That's a lie. You'll probably feel worse, at least in the beginning.

Do it simply because you love life and want to stay around as long as possible.

If you are worried about how long it will be before you stop wanting a cigarette during that "kick off your shoes and have a drink after work" time, look at it this way: Life is a series of trade-offs, big and little. This one is big.

—*Faith B. Tingley*

Source: Faith B. Tingley, *New York Times*, 21 February 1988, sec. 1, pp. 23–24.

FIGURE 6.5
You Can Do It!

Did You Know That . . .

The state with highest percentage of former smokers (20 percent) is Maine.

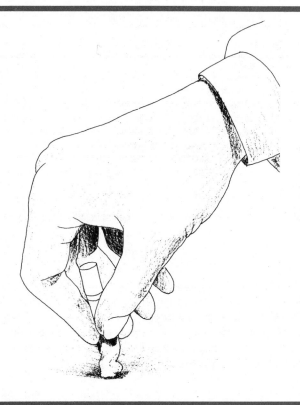

Kicking the smoking habit is rarely easy, but the rewards will last you a lifetime!

list of the possible programs that can help you and then choose an approach. Some therapies, such as Smoker's Anonymous, are free. Others are more costly, but you may find a way to cover the expense. If you work for a corporation, ask if they fund a quit-smoking program. Many of them do and will be happy to help foot the bill if it means having one fewer employee who smokes.

In the meantime, get a head start by changing some behavior that you normally associate with smoking. Try eating meals in the non-smoking section of restaurants if you normally smoke after meals. Start exercising more regularly—the extra activity

Table 6.1 Estimated Savings from Quitting

Packs Per Day	Years Smoking								
	5	10	15	20	25	30	35	45	50
$1/2$	1,916.25	3,832.50	5,748.75	7,665.00	9,581.25	11,497.50	13,413.75	17,246.25	19,162.50
1	3,832.50	7,665.00	11,497.50	15,330.00	19,162.50	22,995.00	26,827.50	34,492.50	38,325.00
$1^1/2$	5,748.75	11,497.50	17,246.25	22,995.00	28,743.75	34,492.50	40,241.25	51,738.75	57,487.50
2	7,665.00	15,330.00	22,995.00	30,660.00	38,325.00	45,990.00	53,665.00	68,985.00	76,650.00
$2^1/2$	9,581.25	19,162.50	28,743.75	38,325.00	47,906.25	57,487.50	67,068.75	86,231.25	95,812.50
3	11,497.50	22,995.00	34,492.50	45,990.00	57,487.50	68,985.00	80,482.50	103,477.50	114,975.00
$3^1/2$	13,413.75	26,827.50	40,241.25	53,665.00	67,068.75	80,482.50	93,896.25	120,723.75	134,137.50
4	15,330.00	30,660.00	45,990.00	61,320.00	76,650.00	91,980.00	107,310.00	137,970.00	153,300.00
$4^1/2$	17,246.25	34,492.50	51,738.75	68,985.00	86,231.25	103,477.50	120,723.75	155,216.25	172,462.50

This chart, based on a cigarette package cost of $2.10, shows how much you can save by kicking the habit.

will keep you busier and can become as pleasurable a pastime as smoking without the health hazards. Keep a container or a piggy bank to collect the money you would normally spend on cigarettes; one of the best things about kicking the smoking habit is that it will make you richer. Most important, keep up your resolve. If you suffer a relapse or start smoking again, don't be discouraged. Remember, kicking any addiction is not easy, but the rewards to reap are plentiful. W

Glossary

A

Abstinence: The total avoidance of a specific substance, such as alcohol or tobacco.

Acetylcholine: A type of neurotransmitter that is thought to play a role in the nerve centers for thought and higher mental function.

Acupuncture: Chinese system of inserting needles at various "pressure points" on the body; unproven as a smoking-cessation device.

Addictive: Capable of inducing a compulsive physiological or psychological need.

Adolescence: The period of intense change that marks the transition between childhood and adulthood.

Alcoholics Anonymous (AA): An organization founded by two alcoholics in the 1930s; dedicated to helping others fight alcohol addiction through regular meetings and a specific 12-step program.

Alveoli: Tiny air sacs in the lungs.

Alzheimer's disease: A degenerative disease of the central nervous system, characterized by prematurely senile mental deterioration.

American Bar Association (ABA): An organization comprised of practicing American lawyers.

Angina: Heart pain caused by lack of blood flow.

Antidepressant: Medication used to relieve or prevent psychological depression.

Apoplexy: Stroke.

Arteriosclerosis: A group of disorders that causes thickening and loss of elasticity of artery walls.

B

Behavior modification: The application of certain conditioning techniques to modify or control behavior.

Bronchial tree: The branched, hollow tubing that connects breathing passages from the mouth and nose to the lungs.

Bronchitis: Acute or chronic inflammation of the bronchial tubes.

Bubonic plague: A contagious, deadly disease characterized by uncontrolled lymph node swelling.

C

Capillary: A vessel that carries blood between the arteries and veins.

Carbon dioxide: A colorless, odorless gas present in air and produced as a by-product of the bodily metabolic process.

Carbon monoxide: A colorless, odorless toxic gas present in engine exhaust and cigarette smoke.

Carboxyhemoglobin: A combination of hemoglobin and carbon monoxide, which forms in the blood when carbon monoxide is inhaled so that the blood is unable to combine with oxygen.

Carcinogens: Cancer-causing agents.

Cardiovascular: Of the heart and blood vessels.

Cessation: A stop; the temporary or permanent ceasing of a habit such as smoking.

Chronic obstructive lung disease (COLD): Any of a series of respiratory infections, ranging from chronic but usually harmless disorders, such as bronchitis, to potentially fatal illnesses, such as emphysema.

Cilia: Tiny hairs that line the bronchial tubes and transport mucus upwards to the throat by rhythmic wave-like actions.

Circulatory system: The system consisting of the heart and blood vessels which transports blood throughout the body.

Cirrhosis: A degenerative liver disease characterized by the accumulation of large fatty deposits and scar tissue that impair functioning.

Clonidine: A drug used to treat high blood pressure.

Congenital deformities: Birth defects; physical or mental abnormalities arising before birth from either a genetic defect or intra-uterine damage.

Coronary heart disease: Temporary or permanent damage to the heart due to restricted blood flow through narrowed or blocked coronary arteries.

Coronary-pulmonary system: The heart and bloodstream, and all organs and tissue related to their functioning.

Cyanide: A broup of often highly toxic chemical compounds containing cyanogen.

Cytology: The analysis of the structure of individual cells.

D

Deferment: Official postponement of military service.

Dependent: To be in need, either physically or psychologically, of regularly administered dosages of a specific substance, such as nicotine.

E

Emphysema: A severe lung disorder characterized by gradual destruction of the tiny air sacs in the lung (alveoli) and a reduction in elasticity of lung tissue that impairs the lung's efficiency.

Endorphins: A group of substances produced within the body that relieves pain; the body's natural opiates.

Environmental smoke: Cigarette smoke released directly into the air and sometimes inhaled by nearby nonsmokers; sidestream smoke.

Enzyme: A protein that regulates the rate of a chemical reaction in the body.

Epidemiologist: A scientist who researches the effects of disease on groups of people rather than individuals.

Epilepsy: A disorder characterized by disturbed electric impulses in the central nervous system.

Epinephrine: A natural hormone, also known as adrenaline; triggered by stress, exercise, or fear.

Epithelium: One or more of the cellular layers that completely cover the surface of the body.

F

First Amendment: The section of the Bill of Rights stating that all Americans have the right to practice freedom of speech, freedom of the press, and freedom of religion.

G

Genetic diseases: Illness relating to or caused by one's genes, biological elements that determine one's hereditary characteristics.

Gingival: Pertaining to the gums.

Glycoprotein: A chemical found in tobacco smoke believed to affect the size and elasticity of arteries.

Group participation programs: Programs designed to help several people quit smoking through the help of regularly scheduled meetings.

H

Health advocates: Professionals, usually in the health field, involved in actions dedicated to improving the general health of the nation.

Hemoglobin: The oxygen-carrying pigment found in red blood cells.

Hormone: A chemical released into the bloodstream by a gland to produce a specific effect on certain bodily tissue.

Hyperactivity: A behavioral pattern in children characterized by overactivity and inability to concentrate.

Hypnotism: The act of inducing sleep or a form of meditation; has had moderate success as a smoking-cessation device.

I

Independent quitting programs: Programs that provide literature, videos, and other information designed to help a smoker quit.

Intrauterine growth retardation (IUGR): An abnormally low rate of fetal growth and development caused either by undernourishment or a physical defect in the fetus.

L

Laser therapy: The use of a laser beam, which is a device that produces a concentrated beam of light radiation, for certain medical procedures.

Lesion: A localized abnormal, structural change in any part of the body.

Leukemia: Any of several types of cancer caused by an overproduction of destructive white blood cells, which impairs the production of red blood cells and platelets, and normal white blood cells.

Leukoplakia: Raised, white patches that appear on the mucous membranes lining the mouth, tongue or gums.

Low birth weight: An abnormally underweight measurement for newborn babies; may result from smoking during pregnancy.

Lumen: The open space within a tubular organ, such as a vein or artery.

M

Mainstream smoke: The smoke from a cigarette inhaled only by the smoker.

Malignant: Term used to describe a tumor which is potentially life threatening.

Methadone: A synthetic narcotic, less powerful than heroin, often prescribed for the relief of pain and as a temporary therapy for recovering morphine and heroin addicts.

Miscarriage: Loss of the fetus before it can survive outside the mother's uterus.

Mucosae: Another name for the mucous membranes that line many internal body cavities and passages.

Mutation: A change in the DNA, the genetic material of a living cell.

Myocardial infarction: Heart attack; the sudden death of part of the heart muscle.

N

Nerve cell: Neuron; the fundamental functioning unit of nervous tissue.

Neurotransmitter: The chemical that transmits messages between neurons.

Nicotine: A poisonous alkaloid that is the chief psychoactive ingredient of tobacco.

O

Opium: A bitter brown narcotic drug that comes from the dried juice of the opium poppy, and from which narcotics such as heroin and morphine are derived.

Organic: Of, relating to, or derived from living organisms.

P

Passive smoking: The inhalation of sidestream smoke by a nonsmoker exposed to another person's cigarette.

Peer pressure: Pressure placed on a person by his or her contemporaries to participate in a given activity, such as smoking, drinking alcohol, or taking other psychoactive substances.

Physiological: Relating to the physical and chemical properties of living matter.

Placebo: A substance of no physiological therapeutic value; sometimes prescribed for the psychological relief it may offer the patient.

Placenta: The intrauterine organ that joins the maternal and fetal blood supplies during pregnancy.

Platelet: The smallest blood particle.

Pneumonia: Inflammation of the lungs, caused by viral or bacterial infection.

Premature birth: A birth that occurs before completion of the normal nine-month gestation period.

Prenatal death: Death before birth.

Psychoactive: Affecting mind or behavior.

Psychological: Relating to the mind.

S

Sidestream smoke: The smoke that escapes from the tip of the cigarette; can be inhaled by nonsmoking bystanders.

Snuff: A plug of tobacco specifically prepared for inhalation through the nose.

Sputum: A mixture of saliva combined with mucus and other substances secreted by the lining of the respiratory tract.

Stimulant: A substance that increases either muscular activity or nerve activity in the brain.

Stroke: Damage to the brain caused by leakage from a ruptured blood vessel or a reduction or interruption in the blood supply.

T

Tar: A solid residue formed when the particles in tobacco smoke condense. Cigarette tar is made up of several hundred different chemicals.

Temperance: Avoidance of, or moderation in the use of, a mood-altering substance.

Therapeutic: Having properties that cure or treat disease.

Thiocyanate: A substance, found in many foods, that can be toxic if administered in large doses.

Tracheitis: Inflammation of the windpipe or trachea.

Tranquilizer: A substance that relaxes or calms.

V

Virus: The smallest known type of infectious agent; viral infections range from minor conditions, such as the common cold, to fatal diseases, such as AIDS.

W

Withdrawal: The physiological and/or psychological effects of discontinued use of a drug.

Notes

CHAPTER 1

1. Tom Ferguson, *The Smoker's Book of Health* (New York: G. P. Putnam's Sons, 1987), 38–39.
2. "Surgeon General Asserts Smoking Is an Addiction," *New York Times,* 5 May 1988, sec. 1, p. 1.
3. "Remarkable Progress," *University of California, Berkeley Wellness Letter* 6, no. 2 (November 1989): 7.
4. Anastasia Tofexis, "A Not-So-Happy Anniversary," *Time,* 23 January 1989, 54.
5. "No Smoking: A Decision Maker's Guide to Reducing Smoking at the Worksite," A Report to the Office of Disease Prevention and Health Promotion, the Office on Smoking and Health, Public Health Service, Department of Health and Human Services (Washington, DC: Washington Business Group on Health, 1985): 5, and *Dangers of Smoking, Benefits of Quitting* (New York: American Cancer Society, 1980): 10–14.

CHAPTER 2

1. F. W. Fairholt, *Tobacco: Its History and Associations* (London: Chapman and Hall, 1859), 13.
2. Fairholt, p. 15.
3. D. West, "Tobacco, Pipes, and Smoking Customs," *Bulletin* (Milwaukee, WI: Milwaukee Public Museum, 1934), 48–49.
4. West, p. 51.
5. Gideon Doron, *The Smoking Paradox* (Cambridge, MA: Abt Associates, 1979), 5–6.
6. Frank J. Anderson, *An Illustrated History of the Herbals* (New York: Columbia University Press, 1977), 96.
7. Anderson, p. 89.
8. Cassandra Tate, "In the 1800s, Antismoking Was a Burning Issue," *Smithsonian,* July 1989, 108.
9. Tate, p. 107.
10. Anderson, p. 121.
11. American Cancer Society, *Dangers of Smoking: Benefits of Quitting,* rev. ed. (New York: American Cancer Society, 1980), 16.
12. Doron, p. 3.

13. Department of Health and Human Services, Public Health Service, Centers for Disease Control, Office of Smoking and Health, "Reducing the Health Consequences of Smoking," *25 Years of Progress: A Report of the Surgeon General* (Rockville, MD: 1989), 3.

CHAPTER 3

1. Edward Edelson, *Drugs and the Brain* (New York: Chelsea House Publishers, 1987), 26.
2. American Cancer Society, p. 16.
3. Jonathan E. Fielding, "Smoking: Health Effects and Control: Part I," *New England Journal of Medicine* 313, no. 8 (22 August 1985): 491.
4. American Cancer Society, p. 17.
5. American Cancer Society, p. 30.
6. American Cancer Society, p. 30.
7. American Cancer Society, pp. 32–33.
8. American Heart Association, *Report of Ad Hoc Committee on Cigarette Smoking and Cardiovascular Disease* (American Heart Association Document: 10 November 1977).
9. National Interagency Council on Smoking and Health, "1983 Surgeon General's Report–Health Consequences of Smoking: Cardiovascular Disease," *Smoking and Health Reporter* 1, no. 2 (January 1984).
10. Fielding.
11. National Interagency Council on Smoking and Health, "Surgeon General's 1984 Report–Addresses Chronic Obstructive Lung Disease," *Smoking and Health Reporter* 1, no. 4 (July 1984): 12.
12. National Interagency Council on Smoking and Health, "Surgeon General's 1984 Report," p. 12.
13. William Blolot et al., "Health Consequences of Using Smokeless Tobacco," *Public Health Reports* 101, no. 4 (July/August 1986): 360.
14. W. G. Squires et al., "Hemodynamic Effects of Oral Tobacco in Experimental Animals and Young Adults," *American Heart Association, 54th Annual Session* (Dallas, TX: November 16–19, 1981).
15. American Lung Association, "Pipe and Cigar Smokers: Take a Look at the Facts," no. 0882 (November 1982).

CHAPTER 4

1. *Environmental Tobacco Smoke: Measuring Exposures and Assessing Health Effects* (Washington, DC: National Research Council, 1986), 144.
2. *Environmental Tobacco Smoke,* p. 269.
3. *Environmental Tobacco Smoke,* p. 270.
4. *Environmental Tobacco Smoke,* p. 271.
5. *Environmental Tobacco Smoke,* p. 271.
6. *Environmental Tobacco Smoke,* p. 268.
7. *Environmental Tobacco Smoke,* p. 191.
8. *Environmental Tobacco Smoke,* p. 205.
9. *Environmental Tobacco Smoke,* p. 245.
10. "Involuntary Risk," *Time,* 29 December 1986, 64.
11. "Passive Smoking: Beliefs, Attitudes, and Exposures," *Journal of the American Medical Association* (20 May 1988): 1986.
12. K. A. Fackelman, "More Cervical Cancer in Passive Smokers," *Science News* (18 March 1989): 166.
13. Nancy R. Gibbs, "All Fired Up Over Smoking," *Time,* 18 April 1988, 66.
14. Department of Health and Human Services, p. i.
15. Patrick Young, *Drugs and Pregnancy* (New York: Chelsea House Publishers, 1987), 55.
16. Dodi Schultz, "Born Under a Cloud," *Priorities,* Winter 1989, 6.
17. Young, p. 56.
18. Young, p. 56.
19. Schultz, p. 7.

CHAPTER 5

1. Department of Health and Human Services, p. i.
2. Les Stanwood, "Our High Schools—Going Up in Smoke," *Life and Health* (February 1990): 8–11.
3. National Interagency on Smoking and Health, "Freedom From Smoking," *Smoking and Health Reporter* (April 1984): 6.
4. *Starting Free* (New York: American Cancer Society, 1989), 4.
5. John P. Pierce et al., "Trends in Cigarette Smoking in the United States," *Journal of the American Medical Association* 261, no. 1 (6 January 1989): 56.
6. Pierce, p. 58.
7. "An Uproar Over Billboards in Poor Areas," *New York Times,* 1 May 1989, D10.
8. "An Uproar . . . ," D10.

9. Shirley Hobbs Scheibla, "Not Just Blowing Smoke: Bills to Ban Smoking Advertising Threaten Freedom of Speech," *Barron's,* 2 March 1987, 11.

10. C. Everett Koop, "A Parting Shot at Tobacco," *Journal of the American Medical Association* (24 November 1989): 2850.

11. Koop, p. 2851.

12. James Brooke, "Nigeria to Ban Cigarette Advertising," *New York Times,* 18 July 1988, A9.

13. Sanjoy Hazarika, "Fighting Smoking, India to Ban Tobacco Ads," *New York Times,* 14 August 1988, 22.

14. "No-Smoking Policy Brings Rift in Kentucky," *New York Times,* 25 November 1988, A25.

15. Koop, p. 2851.

16. Laurie Jones, "Additional Steps Urged to Prevent Cigarette Sales to Youth," *American Medical News* (8 June 1990): 1.

CHAPTER 6

1. Department of Health and Human Services, p. ii.

2. Department of Health and Human Services, p. 491.

3. Nora Underwood, "Taking on Tobacco," *Macleans,* 9 April 1990, 55.

4. Underwood, p. 56.

5. Department of Health and Human Services, p. 427.

6. Sally Wicklund, "Nicotine Gum and Cessation of Cigarette Smoking," *American Journal of Nursing* (March 1988): 332.

7. Jennifer Foote, "Out of Cigarettes and Into Chewing Gum," *Newsweek,* 22 August 1988, 64.

8. "Nicotine Gum a Boon That the Experts Say Should Be Used More," *New York Times,* 28 January 1988, B6.

9. Sandra Blakeslee, "New Drug Therapies Are Being Tested to Help Smokers Quit," *New York Times,* B16.

10. Blakeslee, p. B16.

11. Underwood, p. 55.

Resources

BOOKS

Allison, Patricia, and Jack Yost. *Hooked, But Not Helpless: Ending Your Love/Hate Relationship with Nicotine.* Portland, OR: Bridge City Books, 1990.

This book looks at smoking as a full-fledged chemical addiction to tobacco. Allison's positive no-nonsense approach is based on a strategy she has used to help thousands to successfully stop smoking.

Ashton, H., and R. Stepney. *Smoking, Psychology, and Pharmacology.* London: Tavistock Publications, 1982.

Presented here is an overview of the history of cigarette smoking. The history is revealed through anecdotes to make the book interesting, and many of the critical factors involved in the behavior of those who smoke are summarized.

Danaher, B. G., and E. Lichtenstein. *Become an Ex-Smoker.* Englewood Cliffs, NJ: Prentice-Hall, 1978.

There are several different methods available to help smokers quit smoking. The reader may choose from the methods presented in this book, selecting the one that is both personally satisfying and effective. The authors also address the side effects that can occur when you quit smoking, such as weight gain, and describe a variety of techniques to help alleviate these problems.

Dreher, Henry. *Your Defense Against Cancer: The Complete Guide to Cancer Prevention.* New York: Harper & Row, 1988.

This book provides extensive information on how to avoid known cancer-causing agents in food, water, air, and a host of other environmental factors to which we are exposed every day. Twenty-four pages of the book are dedicated to the the link between smoking and cancer. This chapter, titled "Smoking: The Most Dangerous Habit," presents the known facts of nicotine's powerful effect as a drug, examines what happens when smokers smoke, and presents a detailed discussion on how to become a nonsmoker.

Ferguson, Tom. *The Smoker's Book of Health:*
How to Keep Yourself Healthier and Reduce Your Smoking Risks. New York: G. P. Putnam, 1987.

This book examines both sides of smoking, the health risks as well as the psychological benefits derived from smoking. The author provides information and guidance for those who want to quit smoking, and for those who want to continue to smoke yet are concerned about their health.

Fried, Peter A., and Harry Oxorn. *Smoking for Two: Cigarettes and Pregnancy.* New York: Macmillan, 1980.

This decade-old book still seems timely as it examines the threat cigarettes may pose to unborn children. The authors examine scientific data from hospitals and laboratories worldwide. They also cover the chemistry of cigarette smoke, the consequences of inhaling smoke from other people, and the effects of smoking during pregnancy upon both the mother and the unborn child. The book is easy to read, and the information the authors provide, although dated, is still of value to expectant mothers who want to make informed decisions about smoking during pregnancy.

Goodin, Robert E. *No Smoking: The Ethical Issues.* Chicago: University of Chicago Press, 1990.

The author draws upon both medical and social evidence and uses the method of applied philosophy to examine the risks taken by both smokers and nonsmokers, the costs and benefits of their actions, and the reasons for policy programs on smoking in public, at work, and in other places.

Halper, Marilyn Snyder. *How To Stop Smoking: A Preventive Medicine Institute/Strang Clinic Health Action Plan.* New York: Holt, Rinehart and Winston, 1980.

Through detailed self-assessments, the program presented in this book helps you identify your own reasons for wanting to quit smoking. You devise your own plan based on your motivations, and find reinforcement in your resolve to quit by following the instructions, tips, and techniques that are included. The Preventive Medicine Institute/Strang Clinic is an internationally known nonprofit organization dedicated to the prevention of cancer, heart disease, stroke, and other serious illnesses.

Henningfield, Jack E. *Nicotine: An Old-Fashioned Addiction.* (The Encyclopedia of Pyschoactive Drugs.) New York: Chelsea House, 1985.

This book discusses how psychoactive drugs— drugs (like nicotine) that affect one's mood and become addictive—have become such a large part of our modern society. The history of tobacco is presented, tobacco smoke is defined, and the effects tobacco has on health are examined. Chapters include "Smoking," "Women and Pregnancy," "The Scientific Study of Cigarette Smoking Behavior," "Effects of Nicotine," and more.

Keller, Janice Phelps, and Alan Nourse. *The Hidden Addiction: And How to Get Free.* Boston: Little, Brown & Co., 1986.

This book covers addiction to sugar, alcohol, caffeine, nicotine, marijuana, depressant drugs, stimulants, and opiates.

Milkman, Harvey, and Stanley Sunderwirth. *Craving for Ecstasy: The Consciousness and Chemistry of Escape.* Indianapolis, IN: D. C. Heath, 1986.

This provocative collection of research and theory explores all the ways we lose control of our lives through striving for pleasure and escape. The book focuses on the many things we can become addicted to—love, sex, food, dieting, jogging, television, tobacco, even religion—as well as substance abuse. The book provides current information about the biological, chemical, and psychological processes of addiction.

Reynolds, Patrick, and Tom Shachtman. *The Gilded Leaf: Triumph, Tragedy, and Tobacco: Three Generations of the R. J. Reynolds Family and Fortune.* Boston: Little, Brown & Co., 1989.

This dramatic saga spans three generations of the R. J. Reynolds tobacco family. As the book recounts, the founder of the Reynolds tobacco empire died from emphysema brought on by years of chain-smoking. Ironically, his grandson, Patrick Reynolds, the book's coauthor, became one of America's prominent antismoking advocates. The book makes an exciting read for anyone interested in the storybook lives of those who created a multimillion-dollar American tobacco company, the wealth the Reynolds family made by selling tobacco, and the resultant downfall of those who let the power and money distort their lives.

Sobel, Robert. *They Satisfy: The Cigarette in American Life.* New York: Doubleday, 1978.

This older book is still interesting for anyone who wants to learn about the history of cigarette marketing from the 1880s, when Americans purchased only 14 million cigarettes for a penny each, to the 1970s, when more than 600 billion were sold at four times that price. Through smart advertising, cigarette manufacturers created a titanic rise in sales in just 100 years, by using catchy slogans like "I'd rather fight than switch" and "You've come a long way, baby." The author also describes the battles to ban cigarette advertisements from television and to have the surgeon general's warning printed on every cigarette pack.

Tollison, Robert D., ed. *Clearing the Air: Perspectives on Environmental Tobacco Smoke.* Lexington, MA: D. C. Heath, 1988.

Presented here is the hard scientific evidence that lets the reader draw his or her own conclusions about the health effects of environmental tobacco smoke. The editor has compiled the full range of evidence and points of view to provide a well-balanced perspective on the issues of environmental tobacco smoke. Perspectives include those of health professionals, an economist, a sociologist, a labor union official, and a corporate president. Chapters include "Complexities in Developing Public Health Programs," "Cigarettes and Property Rights," "A Manager's Perspective on Workplace Smoking," "Environmental Tobacco Smoke and the Press," "Smoke: A Politician's Angle," and more.

U.S. Surgeon General's Office. *The Health Consequences of Smoking: Nicotine Addiction, A Report of the Surgeon General, 1988.* Washington, DC: Government Printing Office, 1988.

This 20th report of the surgeon general provides important evidence concerning the serious health risks associated with tobacco use. Evidence and conclusions are presented in this report.

U.S. Surgeon General's Office. *Reducing the Health Consequences of Smoking: 25 Years of Progress, A Report of the Surgeon General, 1989.* Washington, DC: Government Printing Office, 1989.

In the 25 years since the publication of the landmark report of the Surgeon General's Advisory Committee on Smoking and Health, substantial changes have occurred in scientific knowledge and public awareness of the health hazards of smoking, in the numbers of people using tobacco, in the availability of programs to help smokers quit, and in the number of policies that encourage the development of non-smoking areas to protect nonsmokers from exposure to tobacco smoke. This report examines these topics and presents its conclusions on tobacco use.

NEWSLETTERS

Harvard Health Letter is published monthly as a nonprofit service by the Department of Continuing Education, Harvard Medical School, in association with Harvard University Press. The letter has the goal of interpreting health information for general readers in a timely and accurate fashion. A one-year subscription is $21. Write to the Harvard Medical School Letter, 79 Garden Street, Cambridge, MA 02138, or call customer service at (617) 495-3975.

Healthline is published monthly by Healthline Publishing, Inc. The letter is intended to educate readers about ways to help themselves avoid illness and live longer, healthier lives. A one-year subscription is $19, or $34 for two years. Write to Healthline, C. V. Mosby Company, 11830 Westline Industrial Drive, St. Louis, MO 63146-3318, or call (800) 325-4177 (ext. 351).

Johns Hopkins Medical Letter, Health After 50 is published monthly by Medletter Associates, Inc., and covers a variety of topics related to healthful living. A one-year subscription is $20. Write to Johns Hopkins Medical Letter, P.O. Box 420179, Palm Coast, FL 32142.

University of California Berkeley Wellness Letter is published monthly and covers many topics, including nutrition, fitness, and stress management. A one-year subscription is $20. Write to University of California, Berkeley Wellness Letter, P.O. Box 420148, Palm Coast, FL 32142.

PERIODICALS

FDA Consumer is published 10 times a year by the Food and Drug Administration, U.S. Public Health Service, Department of Health and Human Services. This magazine provides a half-dozen feature articles on a wide range of topics related to health, health care and health-care

products, medicines, medical technologies, diseases, food safety, and so on. Regular columns include brief Updates; an AIDS Page; Investigator's Reports exposing frauds, public health concerns, etc.; and Summaries of Court Actions that provide information on drugs, medical services and devices, foods, and even veterinary drugs that have come under the scrutiny of the law.

Health Magazine is published 10 times a year by Family Media, Inc. This magazine also features a half-dozen articles per issue on fitness for both mind and body, environmental topics, sporting activities, health, and food. It has a regular Healthline section dealing with topics related to behavior, medical information, and children's health. A one-year subscription is $19.95. Write to Health Magazine, Subscription Dept., P.O. Box 420030, Palm Coast, FL 32142-0030, or call (800) 423-1780; in Florida (800) 858-0095.

In Health Magazine is published 6 times a year and provides articles on a number of health issues. In addition to recipes and practical nutrition tips, the magazine regularly includes self-help resources for consumers. A one-year subscription is $18. Write to In Health, P.O. Box 52431, Boulder, CO 80321-2431.

Priorities: For Long Life & Good Health is published quarterly by the American Council of Science and Health, Inc. (ACSH), a nonprofit consumer education association promoting scientifically balanced evaluations of nutrition, chemicals, life-style factors, the environment, and human health. General individual membership in ACSH, which includes a subscription to *Priorities,* costs $25 a year. Write to the Subscription Department, Priorities, 1995 Broadway, 16th Floor, New York, NY 10023-5860.

HOTLINES

Cancer Information Service, (800) 4-CANCER. When you call this number you will reach a computer recording that will then direct you to push a number on your touch-tone phone. You can choose to speak with one of the specially trained counselors, order publications, or both. Prerecorded messages and counselors speak both English and Spanish.

National Health Information Center, Department of Health and Human Services, (800)

336-4797. Operated by the Office of Disease Prevention and Health Promotion, this information and referral center's trained personnel will direct you to the organization or government agency that can assist you with your health question, whether it's about high blood pressure, cancer, fitness, or any other topic. Available 9:00 A.M. to 5:00 P.M., Eastern Standard Time, Monday through Friday.

Tel-Med is a free telephone service provided in many cities. You can call and ask for a specific tape number, and have the health message played for you over the phone. There are over 300 medical topics to choose from, including topics related to maintaining a healthy life-style, and many states provide toll-free numbers for this service. Call your local information operator to find the nearest Tel-Med office, or write to Tel-Med, Box 970, Colton, CA 92324.

VIDEOTAPES

Big Dipper. Independent Video Services, Oregon Research Institute, P.O. Box 5322, Eugene, OR 97405. (503) 345-3455.

This 19-minute video shows the harmful effects of smokeless tobacco. Chewing tobacco is often viewed as a safe alternative to smoking tobacco cigarettes. This has proven to be a misconception. The video explains how addictive smokeless tobacco can be and how harmful it is to one's health.

GOVERNMENT, CONSUMER, AND ADVOCACY GROUPS

Action On Smoking And Health (ASH), 2013 H Street, NW, Washington, DC 20006, (202) 659-4310

This group, sponsored by over 50 leading physicians, scientists, lawyers, educators, commentators, and celebrities, was created to take effective national legal action to protect the rights of the "nonsmoking majority." The organization works to reduce the negative effects of smoking, fight unfair and deceptive cigarette advertising and promotion practices, force the tobacco industry to pay for the harm caused by smoking, and generally work to increase the antismoking message. The no-smoking legisla-

tion imposed on restaurants, airlines, buses, trains, and other public places is partly the result of the antismoking efforts of the ASH. Publishes a bimonthly periodical and a newsletter.

American Cancer Society (ACS), 1599 Cliffs Road, Atlanta, GA 30329, (404) 320-3333

The ACS supports education and research in cancer prevention, diagnosis, detection, and treatment, including research on the health effects of smoking. Provides special services to cancer patients. Sponsors Reach to Recovery, CanSurmount, and I Can Cope.

American Council on Science and Health (ACSH), 1995 Broadway, 16th Floor, New York, NY 10023, (212) 362-7044

The purpose of this organization is to provide consumers with scientifically balanced evaluations of food, chemicals, the environment, and human health. Council personnel participate in government regulatory proceedings, public debates and other forums, and regularly write for professional and scientific journals, popular magazines, and newspaper columns. The council holds national press conferences, produces a self-syndicated series of health updates for radio, and provides 24-hour computer one-line articles featuring commentary, press releases, and questions and answers on health topics. Publishes brochures and pamphlets on numerous health topics and research reports on public health and environmental issues.

American Heart Association (AHA), 7320 Greenville Avenue, Dallas, TX 75231, (214) 373-6300

The AHA supports research, education, and community service programs with the goal of reducing premature death and disability from stroke and cardiovascular disease. Publishes several books, periodicals, and pamphlets related to healthy heart management.

American Lung Association (ALA), 1740 Broadway, New York, NY 10019, (212) 315-8700

Membership includes a federation of state and local associations of physicians, nurses, and laypeople interested in the prevention and control of lung disease. Works with other organizations in planning and conducting programs in community services; public, professional, and patient education; and research. Makes policy recommendations regarding medical care of respiratory disease, occupational health, hazards of smoking, and air conservation. The ALA is financed by the annual Christmas Seal

Campaign and other fund-raising activities.

Citizens Against Tobacco Smoke (CATS), P.O. Box 36236, Cincinnati, OH 45236, (513) 984-8834

Membership includes health and environmental organizations and individuals concerned with indoor air pollution caused by tobacco smoke. The organization has set a national agenda to promote a tobacco-free society by the year 2000, and supports a ban on smoking in enclosed public places, restaurants, and work places. Sponsors the Smoke-Free Skies Campaign, which encourages a total ban on smoking on airline flights and in airports. Disseminates information about the effects of second-hand smoke and how to lobby for clean indoor air laws. Compiles statistics and publishes a quarterly newsletter for members.

Coalition On Smoking Or Health (CSH), 1615 New Hampshire Avenue, NW, Suite 200, Washington, DC 20009, (202) 234-9375

This group was formed by the American Lung Association, the American Heart Association, and the American Cancer Society to bring smoking prevention and education issues more effectively to the attention of federal legislators and policymakers. Supports an increase in cigarette excise taxes and the replacement of current health warnings on cigarette packages and advertisements with even more detailed and specific warnings concerning the risks of smoking.

Group Against Smokers' Pollution (GASP), P.O. Box 632, College Park, MD 20740, (301) 577-6427

Founded by nonsmokers who are adversely affected by tobacco smoke, GASP has the goal of promoting the rights of nonsmokers, educating the public about the problems of second-hand smoke, and regulating smoking in public places. Produces an educational slide series and distributes educational literature, buttons, posters, and bumper stickers. Also publishes a handbook called *The Nonsmokers' Liberation Guide.*

National Association of Nonsmokers (NANS), 8701 Georgia Avenue, Suite 200, Silver Spring, MD 20910-3714, (202) NO-SMOKE

This newly formed nonprofit association was founded to represent the nonsmoker. The purpose of NANS is to support and promote responsible nonsmoking legislation, to educate the public about the relationship between smoking and health, and to assist members regarding their rights as nonsmokers. Inter-

ested individuals can become members for an annual fee of $10. Membership dues and contributions provide the funds for nonsmoking education and lobbying for nonsmokers rights. The primary adviser to this new group is Cyril F. Brickfield, the former president of the American Association of Retired Persons.

National Interagency Council On Smoking And Health (NICSH), c/o American Heart Association, 7320 Greenville Avenue, Dallas, TX 75231, (214) 750-5352

Membership includes governmental and private groups fighting cigarette smoking. These groups include the American Heart Association, the American Cancer Society, the American Lung Association, the American Dental Association, and the U.S. Public Health Service. Goals are to coordinate member agency plans and programs aimed at combating smoking as a health hazard. Assists in determining legislative and regulatory policies for the Coalition on Smoking and Health. Seeks legislation to abolish cigarette advertising and require labeling of cigarette packages with health warnings.

National Listen America Club (NLAC), 2686 Townsgate Road, Westlake Village, CA 91359, (805) 497-9457

Junior and senior high school students who have pledged not to smoke, drink alcohol, or use drugs for the purpose of "getting high." Provides a variety of community service projects including an annual national two-hour television special. Projects are designed to promote and recognize the positive and constructive things young people are doing. Publishes *Listen America Magazine,* monthly, and *Tune In,* a biweekly newsletter.

Office on Smoking and Health, Technical Information Center, Park Building, Room 158, 85600 Fishers Lane, Rockville, MD 20857, (301) 443-1690

Offers bibliographic and reference service to researchers and others and publishes and distributes a number of titles in the field of smoking.

The Patrick Reynolds Foundation For a Smoke Free America, 279 South Beverly Drive, Suite 2000, Beverly Hills, CA 90212, (213) 277-1111

Patrick Reynolds, grandson of the founder of the R. J. Reynolds tobacco company, established this antismoking foundation. Its goals are to support innovative activist organizations working for tobacco control at the local, regional, and national levels, develop educational programs for young people, and fund innovative public education strategies including media counteradvertising.

Smoking Policy Institute (SPI), 914 E. Jefferson, P.O. Box 20271, (206) 324-4444

Assists companies in developing policies to restrict or prohibit smoking. Provides consultation and training to corporate management on legal, legislative, health, economic, and labor issues related to the formulation and implementation of effective smoking-control policies. Issues a Corporate Assessment Survey to assist companies in analyzing employee attitudes toward smoking-control issues. Maintains a resource center containing articles and government statistics on smoking. Publishes a quarterly newsletter, *Health Options*. Also distributes three videotapes, *Let's Talk Smoking Policies, Let's Clear the Air,* and *90 Days to a Smoke-Free Workplace.*

Stop Teen-Age Addiction to Tobacco (STAT), 121 Lyman Street, Suite 210, Springfield, MA 01103, (413) 732-7828

Works to raise public awareness of the roles of tobacco advertisements and promotions in influencing children to smoke. Studies how children obtain tobacco and how to prevent them from doing so. Works in cooperation with merchants to prevent children from purchasing cigarettes. Conducts programs in schools to encourage children not to start smoking and to quit if they have started. Was involved in devising the California law that closed student smoking areas in schools. Conducts seminars and workshops. Activities are currently concentrated in California, but the organization plans to expand nationally. Publishes quarterly *Tobacco and Youth Reporter.*

Tri-Agency Tobacco-Free American Project (TAT-FAP), c/o American Cancer Society, 1599 Cliffs Road, Atlanta, GA 30329

Formerly the Tobacco-Free Young America Project, this organization is sponsored jointly by the American Cancer Society and the American Heart Association and is governed by a steering committee of five members from each group. The purpose is to develop programs to encourage young people to be tobacco-free. Current programs include: Smoke Free Class of the Year 2000 (an attempt to have this class be the first high school graduating class to grow up smoke-free); Tobacco-Free Schools Project, conducted with the National School Boards Association, which seeks to eliminate smoking at schools or school-related events; a clearinghouse of information on state-mandated tobacco-related legislation, specifically in the areas of excise taxes, clean indoor air, and free sampling to minors. No publications are produced.

Index

Page 4 Reprinted by permission of the Putnam Publishing Group from *The Smoker's Book of Health* by Tom Ferguson, M.D. Copyright © 1987 by Tom Ferguson, M.D. Page 6 Figure 1.3 Copyright © 1988 by The New York Times Company. Reprinted by permission. Page 7 Special reprint permission granted by *Current Health 2*, published by Field Publications. Copyright © 1988 by Field Publications. *Current Health* is a federally registered trademark of Field Publications. Page 11 Reprinted from *Smokeless Booklet II*, copyright © 1983. The Smokeless® program was developed by the American Institute for Preventive Medicine, Southfield, MI, 1983, 1990. Page 15 Reprinted by permission of the Putnam Publishing Group from *The Smoker's Book of Health* by Tom Ferguson, M.D. Copyright © 1987 by Tom Ferguson, M.D. Page 22 From *Insight*, May 8, 1989. Copyright © 1989 by Insight/David Holzman. Reprinted by permission. Page 29 Reprinted by permission of Cassandra Tate, copyright © 1989. Ms. Tate is a Ph.D. candidate in history at the University of Washington, Seattle. Page 32 Reprinted from *Priorities*, the quarterly magazine of the American Council on Science and Health, 1995 Broadway, 16th Floor, New York, NY 10023. Page 38 Figure 3.1 Copyright © 1990

Smokeless Program, American Institute for Preventive Medicine, 24450 Evergreen Rd., Southfield, MI 48075. Page 40 Excerpted from the March 1990 issue of the *Harvard Health Letter*. Copyright © 1990 by the President and Fellows of Harvard College. Page 42 Table 3.1 Reprinted by permission of the Putnam Publishing Group from *The Smoker's Book of Health* by Tom Ferguson, M.D. Copyright © 1987 by Tom Ferguson, M.D. Page 46 Copyright © 1990 by The New York Times Company. Reprinted by permission. Page 51 Copyright © 1988 by The New York Times Company. Reprinted by permission. Page 55 Reprinted with permission from Dr. C. Everett Koop. Page 58 Reprinted with permission from the World Health Organization. Page 62 Reprinted with permission from Alan H. Gross, M.D., F.C.C.P. Page 65 Copyright © 1990 by The New York Times Company. Reprinted by permission. Page 67 From *Newsweek*, June 11, 1990. Copyright © 1990, Newsweek, Inc. All rights reserved. Reprinted by permission. Page 69 Copyright © 1987 by the AAAS. Page 74 Copyright © 1989 by The New York Times Company. Reprinted by permission. Page 78 Reprinted from *Priorities*, the quarterly magazine of the American Council on Science and Health, 1995 Broadway, 16th Floor, New York, NY 10023.

Page 84 Reprinted by permission of Beth Levine. Page 93 Reprinted by permission of The Alcohol Research Information Service. Page 95 Copyright © 1989 by The New York Times Company. Reprinted by permission. Page 98 Copyright © 1990, American Medical News. Reprinted with permission. Page 100 Reprinted from *Priorities*, the quarterly magazine of the American Council on Science and Health, 1995 Broadway, 16th Floor, New York, NY 10023. Page 105 Copyright © 1990 by The New York Times Company. Reprinted by permission. Page 109 From the *American Medical Association Family Medical Guide* by the American Medical Association. Copyright © 1982 by The American Medical Association. Reprinted by permission of Random House, Inc. Page 111 Reprinted with permission from The American Cancer Society, Inc. Page 113 Copyright © 1991 by News America Publishing Incorporated. All rights reserved. Reprinted with the permission of *New York* Magazine. Page 118 Reprinted by permission from *Changing Times*, the Kiplinger Magazine, October 1989 issue. Copyright © 1989 by the Kiplinger Washington Editors, Inc. Page 123 Copyright © 1988 by The New York Times Company. Reprinted by permission.